The Lie Detectives
In Search of a Playbook
for Winning Elections in
the Disinformation Age

COLUMBIA GLOBAL REPORTS
NEW YORK

The Lie Detectives

In Search of a Playbook for Winning Elections in the Disinformation Age

Sasha Issenberg

Gabon

Philippines

© 2023 Jeffrey L. Ward

Published by Columbia Global Reports
91 Claremont Avenue, Suite 515
New York, NY 10027
globalreports.columbia.edu
facebook.com/columbiaglobalreports
@columbiaGR

Library of Congress Cataloging-in-Publication Data
Names: Issenberg, Sasha, author.
Title: The lie detectives : in search of a playbook for winning elections in the
    disinformation age / [Sasha Issenberg].
Description: [New York] : [Columbia Global Reports], [2024] | Includes
    bibliographical references.
Identifiers: LCCN 2023038244 (print) | LCCN 2023038245 (ebook) |
    ISBN 9798987053621 (pbk) | ISBN 9798987053638 (ebk)
Subjects: LCSH: Disinformation—Political aspects—United States. | Internet in
    political campaigns—United States. | Political campaigns—United States. | Political
    campaigns—Technological innovations—United States. | Political campaigns—
    United States—Psychological aspects.
Classification: LCC JA85.2.U6 I77 2024 (print) | LCC JA85.2.U6 (ebook) |
    DDC 324.973—dc23/eng/20230912
LC record available at https://lccn.loc.gov/2023038244
LC ebook record available at https://lccn.loc.gov/2023038245

Cover design by Kelly Winton
Interior design by Strick&Williams
Map design by Jeffrey L. Ward
Author photograph by Amy Levin

Printed in the United States of America

To my daughter, Maximilia Luda Issenberg,
may you live in less interesting times

CONTENTS

10   CAST OF CHARACTERS

Listed in order of appearance.

Jeremy Rosner
Pollster and international campaign
consultant, Greenberg Quinlan
Rosner Research

**Greenberg Quinlan Rosner
Research**
Washington-based political
consulting firm specializing in
polling and digital strategy

Media Matters for America
Progressive nonprofit organization
dedicated to tracking conservative
media

Jiore Craig
Digital strategist, Greenberg
Quinlan Rosner Research

Will Robinson
Democratic media consultant

Dmitri Mehlhorn
donor adviser to Reid Hoffman

Reid Hoffman
LinkedIn founder and major donor
to Democratic candidates and
causes

Matt Osborne
Alabama-based writer and
progressive political consultant

Angus King
United States senator from Maine,
member of Select Committee on
Intelligence

Cheri Bustos
United States congresswoman
from Illinois, chair of Democratic
Congressional Campaign
Committee

Disinformation Task Force
Unit within the Democratic
Congressional Campaign
Committee focused on tracking
disinformation

Ben Block
Senior adviser for
counter-disinformation strategy,
Democratic Congressional
Campaign Committee

Tim Durigan
Lead counter-disinformation
analyst, Democratic National
Committee

Rob Flaherty
Digital director, Biden for
President

Rebecca Rinkevich
Director of rapid response, Biden
for President

Bully Pulpit Interactive
Washington-based political
consulting firm specializing in
digital advertising

Jessica Reis
Pollster, Bully Pulpit Interactive

David Goldstein
Founder, We Defend Truth

Beau Elliot
Online content creator, We Defend
Truth

TruthNotLies
Anti-Trump super PAC founded
in 2020

We Defend Truth
Nonprofit organization
committed to confronting
digital misinformation, formerly
TruthNotLies

Superior Electoral Court
Judicial and regulatory
agency overseeing Brazilian
elections

Alexandre de Moraes
Brazilian Supreme Court justice
and president of Superior Electoral
Court

Gabriel Gallindo
Media consultant to left-wing
Brazilian candidates

Caio Tendolini
Brazilian political activist

Someone Is Wrong on the Internet

In the fall of 2012 I published a book entitled *The Victory Lab: The Secret Science of Winning Campaigns.* It covered what I considered a scientific revolution that had taken place, largely out of sight, across American electoral politics over the first decade of the new century. Two twin strands of innovation—an influx of new data and statistical modeling techniques to profile individual voters, and the use of randomized control trials to test the effectiveness of campaign tactics—had emerged, informed by methods borrowed from consumer finance and the social sciences. Together they dramatically expanded the toolbox of campaign operatives and forced them to rethink many of their assumptions about how to know what worked.

When I was on tour promoting the book, I noticed that I repeatedly faced a version of the same question from readers and interviewers. I had just described all the state-of-the-art methods that had been developed for identifying and targeting individual voters, and for measuring what actually worked in trying to persuade and motivate them. I had explained how candidates,

party organizations, labor unions, and political action commit-   13
tees were using them to make campaigns more efficient and effective. So, the question would go, what are the scoundrels doing
with this knowledge?

I, too, had often asked this during the two years I spent
reporting on the subculture of self-described geeks who had
begun to change the way electoral politics worked in the United
States. Tea Party groups had begun to raise alarms about alleged
instances of voter fraud in Barack Obama's election; in 2010,
they became more aggressive in efforts to confront it. Yet I did
not uncover much in the way of innovation in how activists used
speeches to promote myths of illegal voters being trafficked
from state to state ("might as well be Harry Potter's invisible
Knight Bus, because no one can prove it exists," wrote *The New
York Times*) or dispatch unauthorized "election observers" to
surveil polling places in minority neighborhoods. These were
disturbing instances of misinformation and intimidation that
could possibly qualify as voter suppression. But compared to
what I saw from the social psychologists developing sophisticated statistical models to predict voter behavior, I was struck
by how refreshingly old-fashioned it all was.

That changed for me in October 2016, when, along with
my Bloomberg colleague Josh Green, I traveled to San Antonio,
to spend a few days with Donald Trump's digital operation,
for what became a *Businessweek* cover story. What many readers found the most newsworthy was a quote we attributed to
a senior campaign official: "We have three major voter suppression operations under way." One campaign aide showed
a series of animated digital ads designed to depress support
for Hillary Clinton among black voters, young women, and

14   idealistic liberals. We were informed they would be delivered as Facebook "dark posts," so that they could not be seen by anyone other than those to whom the campaign paid to show them. "We know because we've modeled this," the official told us. "It will dramatically affect her ability to turn these people out."

It was the first time I had encountered someone who spoke the language of modern, data-driven campaigning to describe activities one might consider antidemocratic. (To be fair, I was skeptical that they were actually doing exactly what they said they were, because senior Trump advisers had proven themselves to be liars who reveled in bluster and shock.) There had been good structural explanations for why this type of activity had remained lo-fi, even as other areas of campaigning grew high-tech. A lot of the groundbreaking research was conducted in academic settings, where human-subjects review boards and other ethical restrictions ruled out nefarious intentions, and most of the pioneering fieldwork was done by charitable organizations whose nonprofit status was tied to their focus on mobilizing historically underrepresented communities. Every legitimate political communicator would fear the blowback from association with practices that the media and their professional peers would consider unethical. Even if one did not, just about every campaign already struggles with the problem of not having enough money or manpower to reach all of their own potential supporters: they would never prioritize trying to interact with the opposition.

But Trump was not constrained by shame, ethics, or the traditional strategic imperatives of political campaigns. Overseas governments, intelligence services, foreign businesses, and domestic extremists—and some entities working at their nebulous overlap—certainly were not, either. To them, the internet had established many new avenues for participation in American elections, some illegal and some merely unethical, with no obvious precursors in the era of television ads, direct mail, and door-knocking volunteers to move voters. I thought back often to that conversation with the Trump official in the years that followed, as I observed so much else online that was manufactured and perpetuated with a similarly brazen impunity. Often what proved influential in ways previously unimaginable were not complex gambits to suppress the opposition vote, but straightforward lies to change voters' minds about candidates.

The durability of those lies posed an imminent threat to democratic societies, disintegrating any sense of shared truth. As individual falsehoods began to inform full-blown conspiracy theories—from the imagined child sex-trafficking ring at the heart of QAnon, to the supposed plot to corrupt Brazil's electronic-voting system—misbelief generated adherents who felt moved not only to whisper down the lane but take to the streets fully armed. An existential crisis for the future of democracy was also an hourly test for those who wanted to win elections.

Lies have likely been part of political conflict for as long as either existed. In the United States' first competitive presidential election, in 1800, Vice President Thomas Jefferson was targeted by unsubstantiated rumors on a range of topics, most notably his supposed lack of Christian beliefs and a rumored sexual relationship he had with a woman he enslaved. (In the late twentieth century, historians reached consensus

16   that Jefferson had indeed fathered at least one child with Sally
      Hemings.) The primary vector for these were more than one
      hundred (typically signed) pamphlets and an uncountable num-
      ber of articles, guest editorials, and letters to the editor across
      Federalist-allied newspapers. Because those who had dissem-
      inated the attacks were identifiable political actors, Jefferson's
      backers could respond. "To the slanders against Jefferson the
      Republicans answered in kind—it is one of the most discour-
      aging aspects of our politics that smears invite countersmears,
      with honors as to scurrility and inventiveness about equally
      divided between radical and conservative propagandists—and
      the assaults on the virtue and integrity of the candidates in
      that election have never been surpassed either in their ferocity
      or in their departure from the truth," wrote historian Charles
      O. Lerche.

      The most heavily mythologized modern electoral disin-
      formation in the analog era, against Republican presidential
      candidate John McCain ahead of the 2000 South Carolina pri-
      mary, touched on the same themes. Christian Coalition leaflets
      delivered by mail portrayed McCain as a godless heathen, and
      anonymous phone calls masquerading as surveys reportedly
      informed voters that his dark-skinned child had been born out
      of wedlock. (She had in fact been adopted from an orphanage in
      Bangladesh.) McCain, too, could respond to those he believed
      had wronged him. He even made his rejoinder to Christian
      Coalition founder Pat Robertson—among a pair of evangelical
      leaders whom McCain called "agents of intolerance"—a central
      theme of his campaign in its final weeks.

      No American law requires speakers to always be honest. But
      in the years between Jefferson and McCain, the economics of

mass communication worked against those who would attempt
to use lies for electoral advantage. To launch something untrue
effectively required real resources—in the form of a media outlet, phone bank, or direct-mail fulfillment house—typically in
geographical proximity to the people whom they intended to
reach. Modern campaign-finance regulations required anyone
seeking to influence a federal election to report their spending and label their communications with a "paid for" line. (Even
political consultants who claim they would do anything to win
are chastened by the threat of prison.) People or institutions
with the capacity to reach large audiences typically determined
that the cost of being labeled a liar outweighed the strategic
benefit. Any effort that prized anonymity would likely be limited by the relatively low velocity of word of mouth.

The internet removed those barriers to scale or scope. Lies
could be generated anonymously at no cost and did not need
to originate in the same district, state, or even country as the
candidate they were hoping to damage. A fraudster did not have
to trick a serious news organization into laundering his or her
falsehoods into the mainstream, as was the case during the 2004
election when CBS News's Dan Rather was duped into reporting on forgeries suggesting that George W. Bush had skipped his
military service. Now artificial-intelligence tools enabled anyone to propagate high-quality deceptions, and the most prominent social-media platforms—including Facebook, YouTube,
and Twitter, now known as X—are powered by recommendation algorithms that, by amplifying and spreading content
that triggered an emotional response among users, potentially
rewarded fabrications. A lie could become ubiquitous almost
instantaneously.

18   Not long ago, it had been possible for politicians to believe
       that all it took was resources, preparation, vigilance, and dis-
       cipline to successfully push back against lies. "You've got to
       respond," McCain explained to reporters in South Carolina in
       February 2000. "You've got to have people ready with access to
       all the information as soon as the phone rings, and if you don't
       get into that same news cycle, you've got a problem."
          That was good advice for an era of scarcity in mistruth, but
       it now feels painfully quaint. A popular comic from the car-
       toonist Randall Munroe shows a character sitting at a com-
       puter explaining why he is not ready to come to bed. "I can't.
       This is important," the character replies. "Someone is *wrong* on
       the internet."
          No individual campaign has the objective of educating cit-
       izens, clarifying their misperceptions, or maintaining public
       order. Rather, they have a narrower, self-interested task: per-
       suading voters to their side and mobilizing existing support-
       ers on the narrow schedule of an election season. Those who
       mastered that project became a distinct class in American
       democracy: specialized, private-sector intermediaries between
       politicians and the citizens they hoped to represent.
          Over the last part of the twentieth century, operatives
       emerged as influential players within the political system, and
       occasionally even became celebrities beyond it. Their power
       stemmed from a perceived omniscience and omnipotence—if
       not the ability to move every voter, at least to control exactly
       what those voters saw and heard. In an era where communica-
       tion ran through a limited number of newspapers and broadcast
       outlets, political professionals believed they knew how to han-
       dle anything thrown at them, with research methods to assess

the potency of an opponent's allegation and determine what
response or counterattack would be most effective.

I wondered to what extent could those skills apply in an era
of ubiquitous digital subterfuge? How could a campaign even
know which online lies were a threat? Was there a way to ensure
that fact-checked content would be seen by the same people
who saw, and were most likely to be persuaded, by the original lie? Was it even possible to answer one without just further
feeding the algorithms that gave it life?

A decade after *The Victory Lab* was published, I returned to that
sphere for this book, to explore what had emerged as the most
pressing new research agenda in the campaign world. It is a project defined, and undertaken almost exclusively, by those in the
ideological center and left. The American right has largely dismissed the very concept of "disinformation," believing it to be
(not entirely without reason) manufactured by their opponents
as a rationalization and pretext. "Grassroots conservatives hear
'disinformation' and think it's an excuse to silence, cancel, or
censor them," says Logan Dobson, a former polling and data
director for the National Republican Senatorial Committee.
"Republican operatives like myself hear it and think it's an
excuse from Democrats for why they lose elections."

Those attitudes have shaped into a core policy commitment for Republicans. The first substantive announcement
of Trump's third presidential campaign was a promise to pro-
hibit federal agencies from participating in any effort to "label
domestic speech as 'mis-' or 'dis-information.'"

In *The Victory Lab*, I quoted a Republican microtargeting
pioneer likening his work to an "information arms race" against

20   Democratic opposition. Military (and sport) analogies for polit-
      ical conflict are often tiresome, but this one seemed apt. Two
      well-matched antagonists were investing heavily, largely in pri-
      vate, in search of relative advantages over one another in effi-
      ciency and effectiveness. Throughout the Cold War, two sides
      were preparing for the same type of battle, all while working
      under a set of common constraints.

      But that is no longer the only paradigm. The "industrial
      war" that defined military activity between nations in the nine-
      teenth and twentieth centuries has yielded to irregular warfare
      against non-state actors who do not have to defend land and are
      not subject to the same economic, diplomatic, or cultural pres-
      sures. In the other type of war room, electoral campaigns, too,
      are being forced to develop counterinsurgency tactics to deal
      with the asymmetric threat of online disinformation.

      Unlike other forms of campaign innovation, which were
      shaped by unique local factors like national election laws, dis-
      information presented common challenges to campaigners
      worldwide. In the year following Trump's election, Freedom
      House identified seventeen other countries—from Armenia to
      Ecuador and South Korea—where disinformation and online
      manipulation had played an important factor in elections. Often
      it looked indistinguishable from one race to the next, famil-
      iar lies circulating on the same digital platforms. False claims
      about Dominion voting machines have spread to France (where
      most votes are cast on paper) and Australia (despite national
      laws banning the use of voting machines). By 2022, every dem-
      ocratic nation had endured at least one national vote in which
      disinformation was accepted as an unavoidable part of modern
      electoral politics. (Specialists often distinguish disinformation

and misinformation on the basis that only the former is generated or distributed with intent to deceive. Malinformation typically describes material that leaves a false impression due to
lack of appropriate context. In practice, these distinctions matter little for those charged with formulating a response.) The
element of surprise was gone, but I had no idea what it meant to
be prepared.

I believed left-of-center campaigns were likely to show
us the way. Their leaders had heightened awareness about the
problem, motivation and urgency to find answers, and a culture
of innovation that had pioneered breakthroughs in other communications practices that quickly migrated across the public
and private sectors. I uncovered an international cadre of political operatives who specialized in the "day-to-day firefighting"
against disinformation, as one of them put it. I wanted to know
what she and her colleagues had learned about navigating a
world awash with dangerous lies, and what that meant for the
next campaign.

Fight the Smears

Glimpses of life inside Prison No. 8 in Gldani, a suburb of Tbilisi, were horrifying. Videos showed guards torturing prisoners, including one handcuffed to his cell bars while being raped with a broom handle. "Please don't film this," the young man begged his captor. "I will do anything."

The videos' release on September 18, 2012, had an immediate effect. Thousands of Georgians joined protests against the government, forcing the minister responsible for the country's prisons to resign. Outrage over the videos shifted the public debate in the final month of a parliamentary campaign, and weeks later, Georgia's entire government fell. The United National Movement, whose leader, Mikheil Saakashvili, had been a favorite in western capitals, lost power for the first time since the aftermath of Georgia's Rose Revolution.

That close proximity to an election, along with the videos' murky provenance—in which an unknown third party had paid to provide the material to a television station affiliated with the

opposition—led many to suspect that the Russian government
must have played some role in the episode.

Among them was Jeremy Rosner, a fifty-four-year-old
American who had advised Saakashvili for years. A former foreign policy speechwriter and White House national security
official, Rosner was used to spotting Moscow's hand in other
countries' domestic politics. The crowning achievement of his
government service had been leading the State Department's
effort to expand the North Atlantic Treaty Organization to
Eastern Europe. Even at the ebb of its global standing, Russia
deployed surreptitious influence campaigns to keep Eastern
European countries from drifting too far outside its orbit, especially the former Soviet republics along the Baltic Sea.

Upon leaving government, Rosner reinvented himself as a
pollster, joining a firm founded by Stan Greenberg, who after
helping elect Bill Clinton as president had assumed similar
roles for Nelson Mandela, Tony Blair, and Ehud Barak. Such
overseas campaigns had long been treated by American political operatives as a source of lucrative side work, especially in
the off-seasons and odd-numbered years when domestic business was scarce. Greenberg had a vision for a firm that would
focus simultaneously on domestic and foreign elections, and he
hired Rosner to develop a team to specialize in the latter. The
firm's international work began to differ from the domestic in
a significant way: clients wanted help with far more than polling. Within a few years, it could claim to have run campaigns on
every continent that has known democracy. In 2001, the firm
was renamed Greenberg Quinlan Rosner Research.

24   Despite having his name on one of Washington's most successful political consulting firms, Rosner was a spectral presence in the city where he lived. He did his most important work in a series of far-flung capitals, where he found foreign clients craving exposure to the American experience. But distinctive local conditions in the places he worked—often revolving around parties more than candidates, in which power was shared through coalitions, where staples of American campaigning like fundraising emails and volunteer phone banks were unimaginable—meant that Rosner typically returned home with good stories but a series of experiences that had little application to American politics.

That changed in 2016. In July, on the eve of the Democratic National Committee's convention that would nominate Hillary Clinton for president, a new website called DCLeaks published a trove of embarrassing emails from committee staffers, supposedly the work of a hacker named Guccifer 2.0. The release inflamed existing intraparty tensions and toppled the committee's chairwoman, Debbie Wasserman Schultz. A few months later, Clinton campaign chairman John Podesta had an archive of his own emails published, this time on the website of WikiLeaks, an established nonprofit with a history of publishing secret documents with the stated goal of transparency and accountability. American intelligence officials pinned the so-called hack-and-dump operations on the Russian government, an assessment later confirmed by Special Counsel Robert Mueller. But mainstream American media organizations helped to spread the materials by reporting on their newsworthy contents; some reporters later publicly regretted abetting the Russian operation, but their reason for doing so at the time was that the emails were real, if illegitimately obtained.

Little such ambiguity surrounded the hyperpartisan content from pop-up outlets that proliferated online during the election season, a trend that the *New York Times Magazine* labeled "2016's most disruptive, and least understood, force in media." Many of the most successful posts on Facebook turned out to be plainly false, including conspiracy theories that a junior DNC staffer named Seth Rich had been murdered for his role in the leaks. Some originated from news organizations that were themselves fake. "There is no such thing as the Denver Guardian," reported the *Denver Post*.

In many instances, those creating and managing such sites were motivated not by geopolitics but by economics. BuzzFeed chronicled a group of teens in the small town of Veles, Macedonia, who had concluded that it made sense to create online properties to cater to US-based web traffic, because ad revenues in America were multiple times higher than those originating elsewhere; they created sites like WorldPoliticus .com, which "reported" that Clinton would be indicted in 2017.

A Democrat in the Los Angeles suburbs began creating conspiracy-minded right-wing websites as a form of satire, before realizing how lucrative the work could be. "It was just anybody with a blog can get on there and find a big, huge Facebook group of kind-of rabid Trump supporters just waiting to eat up this red meat that they're about to get served," Jestin Coler, who built a company called Disinfomedia to meet the demand, told National Public Radio. "It caused an explosion in the number of sites. I mean, my gosh, the number of just fake accounts on Facebook exploded during the Trump election."

As the phenomenon took hold, Facebook founder and chief executive Mark Zuckerberg issued a defense of the company's role in the form of a blanket denial with a curiously precise confession. "Of all the content on Facebook, more than 99 percent of what people see is authentic. Only a very small amount is fake news and hoaxes. The hoaxes that do exist are not limited to one partisan view, or even to politics," Zuckerberg posted on the site four days after Trump's victory. "Overall, this makes it extremely unlikely hoaxes changed the outcome of this election in one direction or the other."

Members of the Democratic political class were divided about the extent to which they believed otherwise. But there was a clear consensus that they had been slow to recognize a potent new electoral force in the commingling of malign foreign influence, manipulable social-media platforms, and the weakness of institutions that once policed the truth. Few in their midst had ever before seen anything like it.

"People sort of knew that I had this weird international background and knew something about stuff outside the US, and I knew stuff about Russia," says Rosner. "Everyone on my team was having some of these conversations. Each of our friends were like, 'What is this with Russia interfering in our elections?' A lot of that was familiar to us, and we found that we had a number of skills that we had developed in the international practice that were of use here."

The last time Democrats lost a presidential race, the prevailing storyline among party elites then, too, had concerned lies that had developed and reached velocity out of public view, ultimately becoming too big for the mainstream media to ignore.

In both 2004 and 2016, there were structural reasons for Democrats to anticipate defeat—George W. Bush was seeking reelection as a wartime incumbent presiding over a relatively strong economy, while Hillary Clinton was trying to win a rare third consecutive term for her party—but to Democrats blindsided about the outcomes a disinformation narrative had a deus ex machina explanatory appeal.

On May 4, 2004, ten Vietnam War veterans gathered behind a microphone at the National Press Club in Washington to cast aspersions on a young lieutenant who had captained a so-called swift boat under their command in late 1968. John Kerry had exaggerated his bravery in combat, speakers alleged, and did not deserve a Purple Heart medal and other decorations he had earned before his discharge in 1970. Kerry's service in Vietnam, and his later emergence as an anti-war activist, became a crucial part of his political biography, especially as he pursued the White House while American troops fought in Afghanistan and Iraq. The new organization that named itself the Swift Boat Veterans for Truth, with a reputed 200 members, called that all into question. In a public letter, the group requested that Kerry release his full military service record to "permit the American public the opportunity to assess your military performance upon the record, and not upon campaign rhetoric."

The event received only scattered news coverage, and a day later most attention moved on. But the Swift Boat Veterans for Truth continued to win coverage for their allegations across a farrago of conservative websites and blogs, emerging as a significant force in political communication even as they went largely ignored by the mainstream press. Among the few who kept an eye on the story was Media Matters for America, which had opened its doors just one day before the National Press Club event and scolded journalists like CNN's Wolf Blitzer for failing to identify ties between Kerry's Vietnam critics and Republican officials.

As a press-watchdog group, Media Matters was following a model first established by conservatives in Washington. The Media Research Center had been founded in 1987, with a monthly newsletter that catalogued examples of liberal bias drawn primarily from big-city newspapers, weekly magazines, and network news programs. The group's work helped to institutionalize a right-wing talking point about journalistic bias—ANNOY THE MEDIA; RE-ELECT BUSH, read the 1992 bumper stickers—and, progressive activists alleged, made reporters and editors so self-conscious that they overcompensated in their search for balance.

Media Matters sought to rectify that imbalance by exerting similar pressure from the left. Its founder, David Brock, was a repentant right-wing muckraker with an insider's knowledge of the new conservative media landscape. He aimed his group's scrutiny at ascendant outlets that had barely existed the previous decade. Political talk radio erupted after the Federal Communications Commission in 1988 abolished the Fairness Doctrine, which had required broadcasters to air differing viewpoints on major issues, allowing individual stations to assume a clear ideological identity; voices like Rush Limbaugh and Michael Savage reached national audiences through syndication networks. The Fox News Channel, which was founded in 1996, brought a similar sensibility to twenty-four-hour cable news; it first surpassed CNN in ratings in 2002. As Media

Matters documented obsessively in blog posts, those outlets helped keep the attacks on Kerry's Vietnam service alive when mainstream journalists chose to ignore them.

On August 5, the Swift Boat Veterans for Truth began airing a television ad in small broadcast markets in Ohio, Wisconsin, and West Virginia. The thirty-second video featured a parade of naval veterans attacking the Democratic nominee, including one who claimed, "John Kerry lied to get his Bronze Star." Kerry's campaign dismissed the allegations, noting that none of the men had actually served with him or had any firsthand knowledge of the events in question. But even though the ad itself likely reached few voters—the $550,000 ad buy across three states was a relatively minor investment by presidential-campaign standards—Kerry's campaign did not encourage the mainstream press to ignore it. Communications advisers provided journalists an eighteen-page research dossier they hoped would be used to debunk the ad's claims, while campaign lawyers took those same facts and arguments to local television stations with a request to stop airing the group's material. (Even then, Kerry refused to release his full military service record because, according to one campaign official, he was embarrassed to have his academic transcript made public, as it showed his grades as a Yale University undergraduate were negligibly worse than Bush's.)

Now it was a conflict between legitimate political actors, which moved baseless allegations into the realm of newsworthy controversy. "Back then, everybody would say—and there were a lot of people on the campaign saying this—'Don't respond, you're gonna make it a bigger story,'" recalls communications director Stephanie Cutter. "It blew up because they were able

30   to go on air, and it made its way into mainstream media. They reported this more as a 'He Said, She Said' type of situation, which continued to put the misinformation out there." The story came to dominate the otherwise quiet month of August, as Kerry claimed the ads were Bush's handiwork and the Swift Boat Veterans used the attention to raise money for more ads. By the end of the month, a *Time* poll showed 77 percent of Americans had seen the ads or heard about them.

The consensus among many Democratic elites that the episode had played a role in Kerry's defeat gave a lift to Media Matters, which saw its revenue double from 2004 to 2005 despite the fact that much political giving tends to drop off in non-election years. "People saw that failure," says Julie Millican, who joined Media Matters in the fall of 2004 straight out of college, where she had written her senior thesis exploring links between exposure of the Swift Boat ads and voter belief in disinformation. "They thought that the media was too credulously reporting on some of these without doing the due diligence — look into the players behind it, what were origins of this stuff, contextualizing it — constantly elevating bad-faith attacks and then demanding the other side answer to that."

Millican arrived at the organization's Dupont Circle office each day at 7:30 a.m. and began by reviewing the previous night's transcripts and video of Fox News Channel programming. Then she and her colleagues would produce reports on patterns in coverage — whether in the form of bias, missing context, or outright falsehoods — and their origins. They fed this analysis back to journalists, in many cases the same news organizations whose work they were critiquing, with the objective of shaping future coverage. "If you give the media the information

about the bad actors they will not amplify or disseminate it—
that was an initial theory of change within the organization,"
says Millican. "'We're going to shine a light on the problem,
and that's going to draw attention to it, and then it'll make it go
away.' It was pretty naive, obviously."

That naivete was a reflection of the era's focus on top-down
mass media. Where just decades earlier campaign marketing had taken the form of hand-delivered leaflets and scattered
notices in newspapers, the emergence of television networks in
the 1940s, and their introduction of nightly news broadcasts,
consolidated the country's electorate for the first time, together
reaching 95 percent of American news consumers. Over the
decades after the first television spot ad aired in 1952, campaigns rushed to reach the large audiences that gathered around
entertainment and sports programming. For decades, the
bulk of campaign advertising dollars were spent on just three
national broadcast outlets.

"The political conversation was almost completely contained inside a very narrow new shelf space. Everything about
our business in the political world was focused on that very limited civic shelf space. Most of everything that people would
understand about candidates, politics, and policy would happen
there," says Laura Quinn, who served as communications director for Al Gore's presidential campaign in 2000.

It was the zenith of what might be considered campaigning's high-modernist period. A political operative could see all
of an opponent's moves as they happened, and even the parts
of a campaign that took place away from cameras—like the
dispatch of volunteers or direct mail—were partially visible
thanks to post-Watergate campaign-finance laws that required

32   itemized disclosure. That mix of transparency and accountability extended to political operatives the illusion of omniscience. One could develop a strategy informed by complete knowledge of an opponent's actions, producing a view of the entire landscape. It was possible to believe in the perfectibility of the campaign craft, or at least an endless cycle of refinement.

After the 2004 election, Quinn played a role in creating two of the most important institutions in the Democratic ecosystem as it embraced a more empirical approach toward campaigning. She was the founding chief executive of Catalist, the left's first independent nationwide voter database, and served on the board of the Analyst Institute, a secret research consortium that brought together academics and political operatives to administer and share randomized-control trials measuring campaign activity. The two institutions together created a culture of experimentation, a conceptual breakthrough that nevertheless delivered mostly marginal improvements in how campaigns functioned. Their success linked Quinn to many of the left's largest funding sources, including financier George Soros and his circle of confederated donors known as the Democracy Alliance.

Campaigns approached the burgeoning digital realm not as a place to rethink politics but as one to which they could migrate analog electioneering methods. Websites were foremost a clearinghouse for receiving financial contributions, where donors could come to give small sums whenever inspired without having to be solicited each time through direct mail or call centers. Primitive social-networking platforms like Meetup enabled supporters to find one another without going through a local field organizer, and decentralized phone-banking and door-knocking tools enabled them to turn any dining room table into a campaign office. To the extent that there was a debate among campaign professionals about how the internet would affect their work, it was between utopians who believed it would permanently reorganize politics by removing intermediaries such as parties and realists who expected it would merely make some existing activities faster and cheaper.

Over the previous generation, broadcast media had splintered beyond networks into dozens of cable channels with increasingly small, often siloed, audiences, and from there to satellite-television services that made it possible for two neighbors watching the same program to have it interrupted with entirely different commercial breaks. Now someone could produce a video without any distribution plan, post it on YouTube, and entrust the platform's algorithms to put it before viewers who never made an active choice to seek out political content.

The unbridled optimism did not last long. In January 2007, as Illinois Senator Barack Obama prepared to launch his candidacy for the presidency, *Insight on the News* reported without any evidence or attribution that the campaign of Democratic rival Hillary Clinton was researching whether Obama had attended a madrassa while living in Indonesia as a child. (*Insight* was the legacy website of a then-defunct print newsweekly owned by the Reverend Sun Myung Moon's Unification Church.) Media Matters chronicled in real time as the Fox News Channel and conservative talk-radio hosts amplified *Insight*'s claim to a much broader audience, despite a Clinton spokesperson's denial of her campaign's role, calling the charge "an obvious right-wing hit job." Technology and deregulation had together collapsed

34   the distance between fringe sources and mainstream journalistic organizations.

Kerry's failure to manage a similar situation three years earlier hung over Obama's response. "We will not be swift-boated," communications director Robert Gibbs vowed. "And we won't take allegations that are patently untrue lying down." Nevertheless, campaign officials argued about whether they would validate a baseless smear by engaging with the details; those who advocated a more aggressive response won out. A former ambassador to Indonesia was tapped to make contact with school administrators; word came back that all its records had been eaten by bugs. So the campaign encouraged news organizations to send reporters to Jakarta so they could see first-hand that the school had no ties to Islamic extremists. "I was kept awake at night," reflected communications director Dan Pfeiffer, "disturbed that a random conspiracy theory mentioned by a Fox doofus with zero credibility could get a major network to fly across the globe to confirm that conspiracy theory."

Obama himself appeared on a Chicago television station to directly challenge what he called a "climate of smear," treating the particular charge with a mix of disdain and ridicule. "When I was six, I attended an Indonesian public school where a bunch of the kids were Muslim, because the country is 90 percent Muslim," Obama told an interviewer. "The notion that somehow, at the age of six or seven, I was being trained for something other than math, science, and reading, is ludicrous."

The pressure from Obama's campaign and its allies at Media Matters succeeded in killing off the madrassa story in mainstream media, with even Fox News repudiating its embrace of *Insight*'s reporting. "The hosts violated one of our general rules, which is know what you are talking about," the network's senior vice president, John Moody, told *The New York Times*. "They reported information from a publication whose accuracy we didn't know." But even as the story moved off television and out of newspapers, it continued to circulate throughout the year, becoming one piece in a broader fiction that Barack Hussein Obama—a Christian who worshiped at a Chicago church affiliated with the United Church of Christ—was in fact a Muslim.

"Rather than vanish, the whispered smear campaign appears to have gone underground, and in its purest form," *Politico*'s Ben Smith and Jonathan Martin wrote in an October 2007 article headlined UNTRACEABLE E-MAILS SPREAD OBAMA RUMOR. "Barack Hussein Obama has joined the United Church of Christ in an attempt to downplay his Muslim background," said one of the emails. "The Muslims have said they plan on destroying the US from the inside out; what better way to start than at the highest level?" The message, with the subject line "Who is Barack Obama," ended with a request: "Please forward to everyone you know."

None of this might have differed qualitatively from the character assassinations of nineteenth-century politicians promoted by pamphlet and amplified by word of mouth, but the new lies were able to move instantaneously across long distances. As *Politico* noted, "barack obama muslim" became the third-most common search including the candidate's name on Google, after "barack obama" and "barack obama biography." In a CBS News poll that summer, more respondents had answered an open-ended question about Obama's religion by volunteering that he was a Muslim rather than a Protestant.

36   Obama's campaign attempted to defend against anonymous viral attacks the same way it might respond to one from
any of his other Democratic or Republican opponents. The
social-networking site MyBarackObama, which connected
supporters to facilitate do-it-yourself campaigning, was reorganized to encourage users to report chain emails that had
been forwarded into their inboxes. There was no evident way
to quantify voter exposure to any particular claim, so the communications and research departments relied on an imperfect
proxy measurement—how many times had they received a version of a particular message—to decide which to take seriously.
A proposal to collect the email addresses of all respondents
listed on the forwarded messages and send out targeted replies
was rejected because campaign leadership "thought it would be
a bad look if we were sending a bunch of unsolicited correspondence to people," recalls press secretary Bill Burton. Instead,
the campaign assembled its research onto a site called Fight the
Smears, partially with the goal of drawing in web traffic from
those searching keywords like "obama and muslim."

Nevertheless, even as Obama ascended to the presidency,
rumors about his secret origins continued bouncing between
established media organization like Fox News, upstart digital outlets like Breitbart News, and homemade email messages. The isolated lies about his religion and schooling grew
into a "birther" conspiracy theory that posited he had been
born in Kenya and relocated to Hawaii (while contemporane-
ous birth notices were placed in Honolulu newspapers as cover)
so as to ensure his eligibility for the presidency more than four
decades later. In 2011, Donald Trump cemented himself for the
first time as a major player in Republican politics by demanding

that Obama produce his original birth certificate. When Obama sought reelection, his campaign treated countering such claims as a core strategic imperative, launching a prominent fact-checking website called Attack Watch, with the tagline: "Get the Truth. Fight the Smears."

Media Matters' strategy for guarding against disinformation strikes was to exert pressure on mainstream journalists. But events kept demonstrating the extent to which that had become an outmoded approach for a media environment in which anyone could be a publisher or broadcaster.

In 2014, the resentful ex-boyfriend of a female video-game designer drafted a blog post in which he scurrilously charged that she had cheated on him, including sleeping with game critics to guarantee positive reviews. Game enthusiasts on the bulletin-board service 4chan latched onto the post as the catalyst to organize an expansive assault on what they considered "political correctness" in video games. Misogynistic harassment, communicated via memes, the perpetually remixable digital images that had become their own online vernacular, quickly delivered real-world harm in the form of death and rape threats and hacked personal information to a number of women in the industry. GamerGate, as the months-long saga became known, represented a new style of "open-source reactionary movement," in the words of disinformation researchers Joan Donovan, Emily Dreyfuss, and Brian Friedberg. "All you had to do was join in the hashtag and you too were part of the movement."

Researchers at Media Matters who wanted to map the lies of GamerGate the same way they did Fox News or Breitbart were shut down by leadership who dismissed it as an online cultural

38   phenomenon too far from the group's mission. "It wasn't considered politically relevant," says Angelo Carusone, who became
the organization's vice president in 2013 after leading a series of
boycotts of companies with ties to prominent right-wing figures, including Trump. "They weren't talking about campaigns,
they were talking about misinformation about voting."

Trump's success demonstrated the extent to which those
earlier distinctions had lost their utility. His candidacy was
boosted by the ferocity of online communities, including the
so-called manosphere behind GamerGate, which had been
organized around matters other than electoral politics. "You can
activate that army," Trump campaign chairman Steve Bannon
told biographer Joshua Green. "They come in through Gamer-
Gate or whatever and then get turned onto politics and Trump."

Media Matters shifted its priorities in response to Trump's
victory. "It used to be simple, Fox News was the gatekeeper . . .
but now there are so many potential bad actors," Carusone said
upon being appointed president of the organization in December
2016. "Now there are places like Facebook who aren't bad actors
but can be enablers of misinformation." Media Matters pulled
employees off of assignments live-monitoring talk-radio and
mainstream news broadcasts and invested in software tools
that could crawl online bulletin boards and maintain posts in
searchable databases. "We could dig and see how far we can go
down the rabbit hole until we could figure out where the story
has been circulating prior to it hitting a point that it was on our
radar," says Millican, who was promoted to vice president overseeing research.

Media Matters was not designed to help campaigns, though.
Many of the political professionals who were dumbstruck at the

outcome of the 2016 election were left to conclude that they had
failed to keep up with major changes in how voters consumed
media. "When we started looking at some of these underlying pieces of information about the electorate beyond just sort
of typical demographics, one that really stood out was where
you're getting your information from," says Quinn. "And frankly,
that's not data that we had been collecting or anybody had been
collecting very consistently over time."

As she attempted to catch up, she sought out Rosner, whom
she had known since they both worked for Senator Gary Hart in
the 1980s. As her questions about digital subterfuge grew more
technical—about how to deal with bots, troll farms, and deepfakes, a phenomenon so new the word had not yet been coined—
Rosner knew he did not have the answers. If anyone did, it was
a twenty-five-year-old in his office who had just returned from
six months in the Bahamas.

American politics was a foreign country to Jiore Craig, but
in the coming years she would become the first person to whom
the most important figures in the Democratic Party turned
when they wanted to solve what they considered the era's biggest challenge. "It was a unique moment in time where everybody who had had been looked to for an answer up until that
point had been abundantly wrong," says Craig. "The fact that
I had to start every race in a new country with the building
blocks allowed me to see things that you couldn't see if you were
only ever using the most sophisticated strategies in the same
format."

The Sort of Thing That Doesn't Happen Here

Jiore Craig had never worked on a political campaign when Jeremy Rosner hired her in 2013. She had been raised in suburban Chicago, the daughter of a high-school football coach in a part of the country where, as she recalls, that makes you "like the mayor." But from an early age her curiosities turned abroad. A high-school history teacher persuaded her to give up cheerleading so she could focus on Model United Nations, where Craig made a point of representing Russia whenever possible "because they break the rules, and I like seeing how rules can be broken," she says. She regularly won awards and eventually a Model UN Scholarship to the University of Rochester. "I've never seen her jittery," says Craig's grandmother Geraldine Lichterman, whose nickname provided Jiore's unusual given name. "She's always been very focused and effective, even if she comes off like a high-school cheerleader."

Craig graduated in 2013 with an international-relations degree, an internship at the European Parliament on her resume, and one overriding professional objective: a job that would allow her to travel. To her surprise, despite lacking any political experience, she was hired that fall as an analyst on the international team at Greenberg Quinlan Rosner. "Experience in campaigns was one of the things I looked for," says Rosner. "But there are also other forms of politics like Model UN that would be more relevant to our practice than for a typical domestic client." Craig received a training in public opinion research, both quantitative methods like polling and qualitative methods like focus groups. She volunteered for every overseas assignment that was offered.

Within weeks, Craig was in Moldova, advising former prime minister Vlad Filat as his center-right Liberal Democratic Party sought a return to power. Much of what politicians like Filat wanted to learn from the Americans was how to adopt the digital methods associated with Barack Obama's campaigns, especially mobilizing supporters to increase voter participation. Barely two years after Twitter hashtags drew people to Tahrir Square, the world was awash in unchecked optimism about the power of technology—usually in the form of American companies—to make politics more inclusive and accessible, and to provide a check on established, centralized power. When she set up a livestreamed town-hall meeting for Filat, the first by a candidate in the country's history, she chose to brand it as a Facebook forum in a room festooned with Facebook logos, even though she and her local colleagues had put on the event with no direct help from the company.

Craig lacked the cockiness of many Washington-based consultants who go abroad with the self-assuredness that comes with having won races in the United States, whose well-financed elections are treated as the pinnacle of tactical sophistication. "The reason it was so foreign to me is because

42   when I would go abroad, I would have to spend a month qualifying myself to be there, like, how could I possibly understand
how to run an election in some other country? And, you know,
how arrogant of me to think that I can."

But unlike many of her older colleagues, she felt at home
online; after all, she had no memory of a world before chat platforms and social media. When she was twelve, she constantly
chatted with friends on AOL Instant Messenger (under the
username SnoBrdBaby12 because "I aspired to be a snowboarder
chick"), which caused recurring conflict with her parents.
During her first year of high school, she signed up for MySpace,
and then joined Facebook as soon as it opened up beyond those
on college campuses. "I was not into the internet," she says. "I
was social. I just wanted to talk to my friends."

When advising politicians about how to communicate
online, she would often begin by reminding them of the impulse
that drives people to social media. They are not logging into
Facebook or Instagram to read news or communicate about
issues, she points out, but to see what their grandchildren are up
to or check how a long-ago prom date has aged. "You need totally
different sets of vocabulary, speaking to presidents, prime min-
isters, people who want to run for election, about what's happening online, depending on their age group, and I really had to
tailor my skills to being able to speak to all different genera-
tions on these issues," says Craig, who in 2015 was promoted to
lead the small digital team within her firm's international practice. "We're all arriving to social media and the digital landscape
from a really different starting point."

In the summer of 2016, while the United States was just
beginning to confront the dark side of politics waged online,

Craig was in Gabon advising President Ali Bongo Ondimba, the   43
son of Omar Bongo, the post-colonial despot who had been the
world's longest-serving head of state. Craig was surprised when
the online platforms she monitored were so regularly dominated
by pro-Bongo messages, even though there wasn't much popular enthusiasm for the government elsewhere. Closer exam-
ination revealed that it was all the product of fake accounts, set
up in Gabon but unaffiliated with Bongo's party or campaign,
generating likes and views that promoted pro-Bongo content to
other users on Facebook and YouTube. Craig began to encounter similar cases of inorganic political activity in other races
across Africa. In many instances the culprits appeared to be a
fleet of political operatives from India's Bharatiya Janata Party,
who after Narendra Modi's 2014 election were dispatched to
other countries as an extension of the country's foreign policy
and business interests. Everywhere they went in Africa, the first
thing the Indian operatives seemed to do was set up WhatsApp
groups that could be used to disseminate rumors among the
local population.

Craig then went to plot strategy with a presidential candidate in Panama, where for years a Spanish businessman
had operated a network of so-called ghost publications, with
names like *Río Abajo Press* and *Tocumen Digital,* from his base
in Valencia, as part of a scheme where he promoted Panamanian
politicians in exchange for public contracts. ("Fake News was
used in social media and election campaigns in Panama long
before President Trump made the phrase part of his daily man-
tra," a local English-language publication observed in its coverage of the case.) Afterward, Craig headed to the Philippines, to
advise a large media company that had found itself crosswise

44   with President Rodrigo Duterte, whose candidacy had been waged belligerently online. To compensate for a small campaign budget, Duterte's team had enlisted volunteers to carry the campaign's message across social media. Many naturally adopted his voice and sensibility, becoming goonish propagandists on a perpetual hunt for conflict.

Craig spent the winter and spring of 2017 in the Bahamas, where the firm's client was the Progressive Liberal Party, seeking another term in power. As happened on nearly every foreign stop, Craig found herself learning from an opposition that was ever more creative in its manipulation of digital platforms for political uses. At one point her clients were worried to see that their opponent's video on YouTube was being watched at an incredible rate, on pace to accumulate more views than there were Bahamians. Craig reassured them it was not necessarily the sign of rising popularity; she had encountered a similar tactic in Gabon, where parties paid to manually bump up play counts on videos, to trick YouTube's algorithm into further sharing them. "Even to think to do that, you have to be thinking about social media not as a broadcast system, but as a marketplace, as a public square, where lots of things are going on," she says. Her party lost the May election, and Craig returned to the Capitol Hill apartment that she often left empty.

Immediately afterward, she got a request from Rosner: He and another partner in the firm, Anna Greenberg, were scheduled to meet someone interested in picking their brains about dealing with disinformation, and they wanted Craig to come along. "I was super burnt out," she says. "I remember being annoyed because Jeremy and Anna were like, 'Come to this meeting with these people and just tell them what you've been doing.'"

She was invited to share her perspective with one Washington audience, and then another—a roundtable at the AFL-CIO, a presentation to representatives of major progressive donors. "I didn't know who I was talking to. I didn't know how important they were. I didn't know where they fell in the apparatus of the Democratic Party," she says. Craig typically began with a basic glossary of online manipulation. Bots were accounts programmed to send out automated posts, usually at a clip no person could match, frequently networked to boost one another. Trolls were accounts run by real people obscuring their identity, sometimes to shape online discussions and sometimes to provoke reactions from others. Suspect accounts were those determined with a probability of 51 percent or greater to be bots, trolls, or otherwise "existing to deceive public opinion in some way," as Craig put it. Bot farms or troll factories were organized clusters attempting to perpetuate such deceptions at scale.

While many of those around her spoke in frightful awe of Trump advisers like Steve Bannon and Brad Parscale, and like-minded pro-Brexit campaigners who had been revealed to use similar online tactics in 2016, Craig was worried but not especially fazed. While some of this may have been new to North American and Western European democracies, nothing she saw from Trump seemed much different from what was taken for granted on other continents. There, media manipulation, untraceable outside money, and foreign influence had all been standard elements of electoral politics well before social media.

In many of the places where she had worked, disinformation was such an ineluctable part of the political process that campaigns had never believed response required extraordinary

46   measures. "If you have a bad actor—and it might just be your opponent—pushing something that's going to hurt you, just get ahead of it and treat it like any other strategy point," she said. "Just because it's on social media or being pushed by bots does not change your strategic response to it. You really just don't want to think of these things as this dark box you don't know how to handle. Just think of it as the same type of prep you do for any type of attacks."

The American political figures she met who were trying to get a handle on it were nevertheless inclined to view disinformation as a discrete problem, a novel intrusion on American politics that could be addressed with the right technological fix. "People just wanted quick solutions," says digital strategist Tara McGowan, who in 2017 founded ACRONYM, a well-funded hub for progressive digital campaigning. "Anytime something catches on, and it appears that it's going to get money from organizations and donors, everyone comes out of the woodwork."

That usually took the form of obsessing over "social-listening" tools that enable campaigns or organizations to see where they or their priorities were being discussed online. "All the commercial offerings in social listening were geared toward marketers, communication teams, or public relations groups—and while they could help in some cases with social media needs relating to disinformation, they were very limited in dozens of ways," says the Dewey Square Group's Tim Chambers, because they were unable to "tell the difference between arson and a natural wildfire."

Often in these settings Craig realized she was the only person not selling something or asking for money; the American world of campaign professionals was heavily oriented toward traditional forms of politics, because that was how it generated its fees. Perhaps that is why, she thought, she described the challenge before progressives more capaciously—not just the search for a single piece of software to solve their problems, but devising a plan for anticipating and responding to internet-borne misdeeds once they emerged, and reconciling that plan with a broader, proactive communications strategy. This had not required explanation when she worked overseas, where politicians usually had a better framework for thinking about such problems. But the specific paranoias of the 2016 experience weighted those she met in the United States with a "fear-based panic mindset," as Craig diagnosed it, that led them to ask the wrong questions. "People kept on bringing me things saying, 'Is this Russian?'" she recalls. "I'd say, 'Slow your roll on whether this is Russian. Why do you even think this is worth spending any time on?'"

The American left felt so urgently that it had to act in the face of this new danger that Craig's frequent prescription of patience—before responding to any piece, weigh the benefits and costs, including the possibility of amplifying it—struck some as controversial. "Everyone just had their own narrow, myopic view, and she didn't have a myopic view," says Media Matters president Angelo Carusone, who attended many of the same gatherings. "But she was brutal to everybody in the room, and super-persuasive."

That August, Craig added a slide to her standard PowerPoint presentation that included data from a report recently published by Harvard's Berkman Klein Center for Internet & Society. The study mapped the online media landscape, based on a massive database tracking years of internet traffic matched

48 to consumption patterns to the modeled partisanship of individual users. It framed a fearful asymmetry. Craig pulled out
the most arresting image, a network-analysis infographic that
resembled a big red and blue blob composed of hundreds of lines
connecting dots representing nodes. Activity clustered on the
center-left, around CNN and *The New York Times*, and on the
far right, around Breitbart, the demagogic and conspiratorially
minded website Bannon ran before he went to work in Trump's
campaign. Some of the most trafficked political content on
Facebook, at a volume that outpaced national newspapers and
television networks, came from right-wing media that had been
built specifically to dominate Facebook and did not meaning-
fully exist outside it. (Western Journal was founded and run by
longtime Republican admaker Floyd Brown; Ending the Fed by
a twenty-four-year-old Trump supporter in Romania.) "Claims
aimed for 'internal' consumption within the right-wing media
ecosystem were more extreme, less internally coherent, and
appealed more to the 'paranoid style' of American politics than
claims intended to affect mainstream media reporting," the
report concluded. "The institutional commitment to impartial-
ity of media sources at the core of attention on the left meant
that hyperpartisan, unreliable sources on the left did not receive
the same amplification that equivalent sites on the right did."

None of that was a surprise to Craig. The publishers and
digital marketers who studied the Chartbeat ranking of
Facebook's most shared links had long since recognized the
dominance of oddball right-wing content. Anyone who spent
time on Facebook as a user, or spent time around those who
did, would have noticed it, too; indeed, jokes about how one's
older relatives had become radicalized there by reactionary

memes had matured into cliché. But the progressive operatives, activists, and donors who came to hear her talk about the
disinformation problem expressed shock when she used the
report's findings to illustrate how structurally disadvantaged
the left was in trying to get its message out on the dominant
social-media platform. "I couldn't believe the way people didn't
know that," she says. "The only way you could not know that is if
you were just hyper-focused on Twitter."

Part of the reason the political class obsessed over what was
written on Twitter, Craig knew, was that their peers and journalists were unusually active on the platform. Craig regularly
pointed out how few voters were. In 2017, Pew Research found
just 15 percent of Americans used Twitter, compared to 66 percent for Facebook. (The sites also drew very different popula-
tions, Pew discovered: Facebook skews strongly female, as did
Instagram and Snapchat, and Twitter disproportionately male.)
That myopia was reinforced by existing social-listening tools,
which relied primarily on Twitter data because the company
made it easily accessible to outsiders.

Increasingly those who wanted to hear Craig's views came
from a Democratic donor sphere that was just starting to see disinformation as a distinct problem. The people already working
on it were largely academics and policy experts, who approached
the topic as a challenge to national security, if not society and
democracy. "A lot of what has been published about myths and
disinformation is coming from people who are not running campaigns," says Craig, "who are all taking a fairly defensive posture
to the issue. Campaigns need to stay offensive."

That summer, Craig was contacted by Will Robinson, a vet-
eran media consultant with vast ties across the Democratic and

50 labor ecosystems who had become especially alarmed about the threat Russian involvement in American politics could pose to progressive interests. Robinson thought Craig's experience would be relevant to a few of his clients, including a US senator who was especially worried that Moscow might have reason to meddle in his 2018 reelection campaign.

Craig realized that, for the first time in her career, her skills would be useful at home. In a sphere filled with increasingly specialized consultants—direct-mail designers, phone-bank operators, broadcast-time buyers, focus-group moderators, digital ad optimizers, volunteer-training coaches—Jiore Craig had become the Democratic Party and progressive movement's first counter-disinformation specialist. "I'm not a disinformation expert," she shrugs. "I just did campaigns in other places."

Craig and Rosner began plotting how to market their services to a domestic political marketplace desperate to buy disinformation-fighting services. "Our approach to digital incorporates insights from abroad with years of public opinion research experience to offer a different take on how campaigns should think about digital campaigns," they wrote in a marketing pitch to prospective clients. "Our digital approach to US campaigns encourages teams to move from GOTV [get out the vote] programs to GOVT (Grow Online Voter Trust) programs that rethink organizing to create online infrastructure that fosters meaningful organic engagement among voters by earning trust and giving voters more meaningful ways to engage with a campaign."

It was a vision that aligned with how Craig had observed campaigns abroad using social media and messaging platforms.

In few other places are paid advertising or small-dollar fund-   51
raising central to electoral politics the way they are in the
United States. (The reasons for this vary, including different
campaign-finance laws, cultural expectations, and local economic factors.) So when candidates and parties were first able to
go online, they did not look to the internet as a place to raise or
spend money. Rather they viewed it as a novel sphere in which to
connect with supporters and have them spread the campaign's
message through their own networks.

But few large-scale American electoral campaigns had
emphasized such so-called digital organizing. Craig suspected
this was in large part because existing consultancies had not
figured out how to make the work of linking supporters online
profitable for them. Most specialized in placing digital advertising, earning commissions each time a client bought an ad, or
running fundraising campaigns for clients. Online fundraising
shifted a digital department from a costly outlay into a revenue center. (It was this logic—that spending on Facebook would
bring in more money than it cost—that inspired Trump to shift
his campaign budget so dramatically away from television and
toward social-media advertising in 2016.) Digital advertising and online fundraising scaled up appealingly, as it did not
require any more labor or equipment to double a YouTube ad
buy on or send an email solicitation to a larger list, but cultivat-
ing and nurturing online supporters did not.

Robinson's interest in online disinformation could be traced
to 2011, when he advised an Ohio ballot referendum that repealed
a measure limiting public employees' collective-bargaining
rights. It was no secret that a libertarian-minded Columbus think
tank named the Buckeye Institute had been involved in promoting

52 the original legislation, just one part of a coast-to-coast chain of like-minded conservative entities named the State Policy Network. But over the course of the successful repeal campaign, Robinson realized how far the institute reached beyond the traditional think-tank work of producing research and analysis to influence a small circle of policymakers. Rather, it seemed to be unusually active online, relying on other groups within the network and an amen corner of individual accounts to reliably promote its social-media content, an almost robotic coordination that functioned as an efficient self-amplification machine. A few years later, similar patterns appeared on Facebook, across an altogether disparate set of issues, and for a while it seemed to colleagues that Robinson was not much interested in talking about anything else.

"People thought I lost my mind. People just didn't believe it because, you know, that sort of thing doesn't happen here," he says. "For me, Jiore was a breath of fresh air. She had never done American politics before. She wasn't contaminated."

He invited Craig to pitch the American Federation of State, County and Municipal Employees, which had given Robinson his first political job in the early 1980s and continued to employ him as a consultant. The union was preparing for the next front in a rolling conflict over government workers' collective-bargaining rights. In September 2017, the US Supreme Court announced it would hear arguments in *Janus v. AFSCME,* in which an Illinois child-support specialist Mark Janus argued the union violated his constitutional rights by forcing him to pay dues. It was widely expected that the court would overturn a forty-year precedent and rule for Janus. Such an outcome would give public employees nationwide the right

to opt out of joining a union, and some of the same anti-labor
interests Robinson had confronted in Ohio would likely gin up a
large-scale campaign encouraging them to do so.

The union, which became Craig's first domestic client, already treated organizing as part of its core mission.
Her research, showing about one-sixth of AFSCME members belonged to Facebook groups that would expose them
to disinformation related to the case, helped document to
union organizers what exactly they had to counter with their
member-to-member communication. "Jiore made clear how
pervasive the disinformation was that was coming to the members," says Robinson. "We're not going to stop it. What we need
to do is compete with it. Because there are no referees anymore."

Some of their co-partisans saw a different opportunity
in that absence. At the same time Craig was teaching many on
the American left for the first time how to defend against such
attacks, others were beginning to wonder why they should not
be using the same knowledge to go on offense. Those ready to
experiment with creating disinformation themselves found
themselves with backing from the biggest new financial force in
American politics.

A Violation of
Our Ideals

The five states that, due to quirks of their history, elect governors and legislators in odd-numbered years have assumed an outsized role in the modern history of electioneering innovation. To political practitioners whose work focuses on competing in even-numbered years, the lull between national elections presents a useful anomaly—a year in which elections exist less for winning than for learning. Virginia and New Jersey, which always come twelve months following a presidential vote, have become an essential proving ground for new tactics and technology, the first chance to learn from the perceived successes and failures of the previous year's contest.

For decades, the national party committees were the organs of such research, converting a pyramid of state, county, and local parties into a field laboratory. But changes in campaign-finance law during the early twenty-first century brought new tinkerers into the fold: large donors, who emerged not only as funders of campaigns and independent-expenditure committees but as

drivers of an innovation agenda whose lessons found their way
back into the parties and their candidates.

In 2017, Democrats seeking to assess heavy investments around party building and various new prototypes for profiling and organizing voters and volunteers were often drawn to Virginia, which had become an essential part of any path their party had to presidential victory. (New Jersey, which had a similar slate of elections that fall, was not as desirable a laboratory because it was not a presidential battleground and had more restrictive spending limits.) But for those who wanted a fluid environment in which to explore how information now moved and what it took to change minds, there was nothing better than an unscheduled election popping onto the calendar in an unlikely locale. "How can we take scale-up expertise from Silicon Valley," Dmitri Mehlhorn said to the Silicon Valley news site *Recode*, "to create platforms that make American democracy more robust, so that after 2020, we are resilient against fake news, we are voting at high levels, [and] we are voting in an enlightened way?"

As November 2016 approached, Mehlhorn had had an idea to hedge what he expected would be his disappointment as a citizen with his potential gain as an investor. Mehlhorn, the forty-five-year-old son of a Jewish refugee from Nazi Germany, claimed a grim prescience about Donald Trump's potential from early in his candidacy. Just before the election, Mehlhorn put some of his portfolio into a short bet on public-capital markets under the assumption they would react negatively to a Trump victory. Trump won, but other investors did not panic. Mehlhorn lost money as a result and began to restructure his

56   career so that his financial bets would align with his desired political outcomes.

A few weeks after Trump took office, Mehlhorn reconnected with Reid Hoffman, whom he had first met through an education-reform advocacy group that he led. Hoffman was an early internet entrepreneur who, after a stint as an executive at PayPal, founded LinkedIn in 2002; while running the professional-networking platform, he remained an active investor in other start-ups through a venture-capital firm where he served as a partner. Even as he harbored aspirations to "strengthen public intellectual culture," like many in Silicon Valley he kept his distance from partisan politics. There is no record of him giving to any candidate to federal office until 2007, and over the following five years he backed only four candidates other than Barack Obama.

But Trump's election changed that. Earlier in 2016, the sale of LinkedIn to Microsoft left Hoffman flush with cash and new ambition. (*Forbes* estimated his net worth at more than $3 billion.) He turned to Mehlhorn, a former antitrust lawyer and angel investor in health-technology start-ups, to be the vehicle for his arrival into the national political scene. He wanted to contain Trump, along with the movement Trump appeared to lead, as a civic hazard. Fighting disinformation was a big part of what he thought would be necessary to accomplish it. "Reid really believes in the long-term future of humanity, he wants to make bets that make humanity better. And he believed," Mehlhorn explains, "that the titans of Silicon Valley, including the titans of social media, were part of the engine that enabled Trump's rise. And so they had a special obligation to manage the fallout."

Mehlhorn liked to speak in world-historical terms about the crisis his country now faced, often dipping into a scholarly literature about totalitarianism to justify his sense that the day's partisan conflict had existential stakes and required extraordinary measures. But the duty of dispensing Hoffman's money put him in a position that required bridging the abstract and the concrete.

The most basic description of his role was "donor adviser," a job title that had replicated across LinkedIn profiles in the new century. Over that time, all sorts of novel paths for giving had opened up, notably the super PACs created in 2010 when the Supreme Court's *Citizens United vs. Federal Election Commission* ruling removed limits on independent spending by individuals, companies, and labor unions. But the new landscape was often too complicated for wealthy donors, who typically prioritized their businesses or leisure time, to navigate themselves. Donor advisers served as sherpas, employed by family offices or paid as consultants, hearing pitches from candidates and causes and recommending the ones deserving of support.

Mehlhorn, however, thought of his work for Hoffman less as advising on philanthropic strategy than as developing an industrial policy. Together they created Investing in US, which Mehlhorn described as the "risk-capital or growth-capital arm of the resistance." The company's "central thesis," Hoffman explained, was "that technology is changing politics faster than politics is adapting to technology," and that traditional party organizations had failed to keep up. Unlike some major progressive donors, whose decisions are guided in part by the tax benefits of supporting nonprofit causes, Hoffman brought to his giving both the impatience and profligacy of venture capital. He

58   entrusted Mehlhorn to identify the best options for maximiz-
ing the immediate political impact of each dollar.

Where a typical venture capitalist might see 1,000 pitches
before investing in one, Mehlhorn was far more aggressive,
moving ahead with perhaps one out of every fifteen. At times
that meant donating to an established charity; at other times
he offered seed money to new organizations looking to fill a
void in the activist ecosystem. When a political operative or
technologist had an idea for developing a new tool that campaigners could use, Hoffman was ready to offer backing as an
investor, even when he would measure his return in electoral
results rather than a profit-loss statement. "My approach to
political investing is the Silicon Valley approach," Hoffman told
The New York Times that September. "Find and back powerful
entrepreneurs."

Mehlhorn divided Hoffman's investments into three principal
categories. The first, called Mobilization, was aimed at converting the activism of the so-called resistance to Trump into votes
and other tangible political outcomes. The second, Ecosystem,
focused on developing resources that would improve the
Democratic party's ability to defeat Republicans. The third,
Narrative, was comparatively amorphous, extending from projects to refine election-season persuasion to ones aiming to
remake the structure of the information environment. (The
largest outlay at first was to fund litigation, primarily against
Trump's administration, with the objective not necessarily of
blocking policy or winning damages at trial, but of using the
discovery process as a fact-finding tool. "Getting things into
the courts means that there will be a truth that will emerge, and

then the news organizations, even the shitty ones, will tend to want to cover it," says Mehlhorn.)

The Narrative category also covered what Mehlhorn characterized as the "social epistemology" problem posed by disinformation. At Higher Ground Labs, an incubator for progressive technology companies in which Hoffman was an investor, addressing it was a priority from its 2017 launch. "It was always high on our list," says Shomik Dutta, the fund's cofounder. There was not much available to political communicators, Dutta's research found, beyond social-listening tools to measure online activity. "It became clear that just letting operators know about what was bubbling out there isn't all that useful," Dutta says. "They also needed the solution."

The marketplace was awash with new businesses promising them. There was Truthbot, created by an online-advertising executive with the objective of developing artificial-intelligence tools that could scan the internet for public social-media posts containing falsehoods and then generate comments that corrected them. MarvelousAI claimed it could do something similar, with what it called "cyborg" methodology.

Other entrepreneurs vowed to fight back at disinformation through novel content approaches. Weird Enough Productions, which had been founded in 2014 to inspire self-esteem among African American teenagers through emotionally sensitive superhero comics, declared a new goal of educating its readers on how to recognize disinformation. At Colorado-based MotiveAI, a former *Vice News* general manager oversaw an editorial team that generated eye-catching, sometimes highly sexualized online posts with the apparent goal of assembling right-leaning Facebook audiences who could be later targeted

60   for anti-disinformation campaigns. "Interventions like this are important to ensure that many online communities who are prone to misinformation or no longer trust legitimate media sources can be reached with real news and good facts that they may not see otherwise," chief executive Dan Fletcher told *The Atlantic*'s Alexis Madrigal.

Many of the new entrepreneurs claimed inspiration from overseas. Curtis Houghland, whose marketing career had chased new forms of social media from online bulletin boards in the 1990s to networking platforms in the 2000s, in the 2010s began to focus on the power of individuals who had developed significant personal followings. Such "micro-influencers," Houghland believed, could be used to push back against dangerous beliefs before they took hold online. He won government contracts to fight extremism and hate speech worldwide, identifying micro-influencers within certain communities, recruiting them with paying contracts, and coordinating the content and timing of their posts. After Trump's victory, he started a new firm, called Main Street One, to market that method to American political clients. "The best antidote to disinformation is large human networks of real people sharing real stories en masse in unison organized around an idea, a brief, a piece of knowledge," Houghland says. "If I'm going to appeal to you, I have to be inside your echo chamber, or have the appearance of being inside your echo chamber."

For Mikey Dickerson, fighting disinformation was part of a broader project of making Democrats more digitally competitive. A former Google engineer, Dickerson became a celebrity in political-tech circles when he joined the effort to salvage the disastrous 2013 launch of the Obama

administration's Healthcare.gov website. Afterward, he took
charge of the US Digital Service, a White House unit meant
to serve as an in-house consulting firm for other government
agencies. He left government upon Trump's swearing-in and
turned his attention to electoral politics through a pair of non-
profits. One, the New Data Project, would develop new campaigning tools and aim potentially to supplant the Democratic
National Committee as the left's central custodian of voter data.
American Engagement Technologies, as Hoffman recalled the
pitch, "sought to develop technical solutions to counteract fake
news, bot armies, and other kinds of digital manipulation and
disinformation." Dickerson asked Hoffman for $50 million to
fund a series of new initiatives under the umbrella of his new
organizations. "We gave him $750,000 to do some experimen-
tation," says Mehlhorn. "Not $50 million."

It was far from Hoffman's most costly expenditure of the
year, but it may have been the most influential.

In November 2017, Democrats dominated Virginia's elections,
winning all statewide offices, including the governorship, and
making such massive gains in the House of Delegates that control of the chamber had to be determined by a coin flip. Hoffman
had spent $3 million there, including investments in targeted
voter contact that put him immediately in conflict with the party's plan about which legislative districts to prioritize. Days
later, Mehlhorn hosted a post-election briefing in Washington
to boast about Hoffman's contribution to the results in Virginia,
and was happy for it to be seen as the start of a broader challenge
to the Democratic establishment for primacy in setting tactics
and strategy. "The only environment in which you try stuff and

62   actually have real evidence about whether it works or not is in an actual election with actual stakes," says Mehlhorn. "And there aren't that many of them before game time in 2020."

The following month, Alabamians were scheduled to select a replacement for Jeff Sessions, the longtime Republican senator whom Trump appointed as his first attorney general. For much of the year, outsiders had taken an interest in the two-round Republican primary only to the extent it refracted light on Trump's new place atop a party still uneven about his influence; in a deep-red state, the Republican nominee could be expected to cruise in a typically low-turnout December election. But once former state Supreme Court Chief Justice Roy Moore emerged from a runoff in late September, the national perspective on the race changed. Moore was the most ideologically extreme of his party's contenders for the office, and Democrats began to entertain the possibility that it might be worth putting out a fight against him.

Shortly thereafter, the nominee's Twitter campaign account @MooreSenate saw a big jump in new followers, from 27,000 followers to 47,000. About a thousand of the new accounts had something in common: profile pictures of pop stars, and use of Cyrillic characters in their screen names and past messages. "They ain't from around here, comrade," one commenter wrote.

At Moore's urging, Twitter promptly took down thousands of accounts. Democratic nominee Doug Jones denied that his campaign had anything to do with the accounts and would eventually call for federal authorities to investigate. "What is obvious now is that we have focused so much on Russia that we haven't focused on the fact that people in this country could take the same playbook and do the same damn thing," he said.

"This should not happen to anyone in this country. We have got   63
to take steps to protect our electoral system."

In early December, Moore was the beneficiary of other unexpected support. An organization called Dry Alabama emerged online, purportedly campaigning to ban alcohol in the state. From its Twitter account Dry Alabama dispensed a mix of wholesome memes ("Help make Alabama dry and stop worrying where your husband is at night"), Bible verses ("Wine is a mocker and beer a brawler; whoever is led astray by them is not wise"), and electoral cheerleading ("Pray for Roy Moore"). On Facebook, Dry Alabama put out a link to a petition asking Senate candidates to commit to join its "fight against the decay of our moral Christian society," and used the platform's advertising mechanism to put the petition in front of Facebook users it profiled as likely to be free-market conservatives repelled by the cause. The page reached three million targeted voters, earning nearly one hundred thousand engagements. "Debates broke out in the comments, with 'piety Republicans' and 'economic Republicans' disagreeing over the issue," marveled Democratic activist and former military cryptographer Matt Osborne. "This limited run was a smashing success."

Osborne, who lived near the Tennessee River in northwestern Alabama, was behind Dry Alabama, which existed entirely as a function of those social-media pages. The idea of such a political movement emerging to support the Republican nominee was not entirely manufactured: Moore was a proud teetotaler with support from religious Baptists who fought for greater liquor regulation, although the issue had not been a factor in the Senate race until voters began seeing the Dry Alabama ads. When one of them, a small-government conservative political consultant named Elizabeth BeShears, saw the petition in her feed, she posted a screenshot on Twitter with the comment, "Y'all's targeting is so wrong."

Osborne took validation from BeShears's outrage at being mistaken for the type of right-winger who would like an online video teaching her how to make a nonalcoholic cocktail like the "righteous mint julep." His entire project had been inspired by the previous year's efforts of Russia's Internet Research Agency to turn Bernie Sanders and Hillary Clinton supporters against one another, only rendered in ideological reverse. "Because Moore has always had trouble bringing the 'business wing' of the state party into his fold, this failure to motivate voters left him vulnerable to social media campaigns aimed at driving this alcohol policy wedge," wrote Osborne. BeShears would end up voting for Jones, although she said the Dry Alabama ads played no role in her choice.

It took more than a year for Osborne's role in the Dry Alabama effort to become public. (By then, Jones was settled in the Senate as the first Democrat elected from Alabama in a quarter-century; the last, Richard Shelby, had switched parties to become a Republican.) "I was willing to create content under a false flag, if you will," Osborne said. "I was willing to trick Republicans into not voting. That was fine with me."

Journalists began poking around Osborne's initiative only after it had been revealed that the Moore-supporting Russian bots had a similar patrimony. They were traced to an Austin-based firm called New Knowledge, which had been founded in 2015 as "the world's first platform for defending online communities from social media manipulation." The firm's chief executive, Jonathon Morgan, had established himself as an expert on the way overseas adversaries organized online, and he was hired by Google and the Brookings Institution to map terrorist presence online for *The ISIS Twitter Census.* As the Senate Intelligence Committee prepared in December 2018 to release a New Knowledge—authored report titled *The Tactics & Tropes of the Internet Research Agency,* journalists began chasing leads about the firm's role in a secret operation called Project Birmingham.

In 2017, New Knowledge had been hired by Dickerson's American Engagement Technologies to experiment "with many of the tactics now understood to have influenced the 2016 elections," as an internal postmortem report put it. The project's stated model was the State Department's Global Engagement Center, with domestic conservatives replacing jihadis as targets for its anti-propaganda efforts. The bot network was deployed to give the appearance that Moore was backed by Russian interests, while Facebook pages impersonated homegrown right-wing opposition to Moore. That illusion was so successfully deceptive that an independent conservative candidate named Mac Watson contacted the administrators of one page in search of their support. The postmortem claimed that the program peeled off and depressed enough Republican support for Moore to cover Jones's margin of victory.

The ephemeral nature of online communication made it impossible for journalists to disentangle the marketing boasts from the reality of what had transpired in Alabama more than a year later. The suspected accounts had already been deleted, leaving them off-limits to forensic researchers, and Facebook did not introduce a searchable library of political ads until the spring of 2018, leaving no public record of any payments used

66   to promote the work. Nonetheless, press coverage was aggressive, with the *New York Times* putting it on the front page.
Throughout the stories were hints at the perceived hypocrisy of those who had warned senators of the "ongoing threat
to American democracy" of Russian tactics at the same time
as deploying them to elect one. (Right-wing media that had
minimized disinformation in 2016 suddenly took an interest, too: "Democrats Ran Russian Bot 'False Flag' Operation In
Alabama—And Media Fell For It," asserted a *Daily Caller* headline.) Facebook responded to the scrutiny by suspending five
associated accounts "for engaging in coordinated inauthentic
behavior." Among them was Morgan's.

When confronted about his role, Morgan tried to dimin-
ish the initiative as a small-scale experiment designed to serve
an academic objective rather than a political one. "The research
project was intended to help us understand how these kind of
campaigns operated," Morgan explained to the *New York Times*.
"We thought it was useful to work in the context of a real election but design it to have almost no impact." He offered hazy
deflections, at times dishonest denials, about specific claims in
his firm's postmortem, telling the *Times* that the bot scheme
"does not ring a bell," and, about Watson, that "we didn't do
anything on his behalf." Morgan's lawyers later disclosed to federal regulators that New Knowledge had in fact spent $1,078 on
Facebook to promote Watson's candidacy.

Morgan's defensiveness contrasted with the defiance
Osborne showed when the Dry Alabama stratagem came to
light, its details unearthed by many of the same investigative
reporters. "If you don't do it, you're fighting with one hand tied

behind your back," he told the *Times*. "You have a moral impera-   67
tive to do this—to do whatever it takes."

The two false-flag operations were different in crucial ways, each embodying a different part of the Democrats'
Trump-era brain. Project Birmingham reflected its ego, as
out-of-state technologists with impressive pedigrees claimed
the high-minded mandate to undertake a rigorous generational
modernization of national technological infrastructure. The
other was the party's id, local activists imagining themselves as
insurgents taking up digital arms against tyranny at any cost.
But the two initiatives had one important element in common.
Both had been funded with Hoffman's money—as it happened,
exactly $100,000 to each.

That made Hoffman the target for media looking to pin
responsibility on someone; it was the first scandal of his period
as one of his side's biggest benefactors. The zeal Mehlhorn had
shown over the previous two years characterizing the technologist's mindset as superior to that of politicians had caught up
with him. Prominent figures in the Democratic establishment
were ready to criticize the particular tactics without hesita-
tion, and also to layer on a moral critique of anyone who would
even contemplate them. "It makes it harder for us to win when
they're doing things that call into question what our morals are,"
Democratic National Committee vice chair Ken Martin, head of
the Minnesota state party, told *Vanity Fair*. "How can we take the
higher ground and say that Donald Trump is a liar when we're
out there doing the same thing?"

Under pressure, Hoffman quickly issued a public apology.
He had first read of the Alabama project in the *Times* article, he

68   claimed, and was most disturbed by the allegation that his money had funded a "false flag" attack involving fake accounts with Russian names. "I categorically disavow the use of misinformation to sway an election," he wrote. "We cannot permit dishonest campaign tactics to go unchecked in our democracy—no matter which side they purportedly help."

He said his political team would draft a policy to restrict its future giving. Mehlhorn claimed an unsentimental commitment to efficiency at all costs, informed by a Silicon Valley confidence that everything could be measurable, in this case through his preferred metric of cost-per-vote. When that mentality convinced Mehlhorn he knew better than his presumptive allies about how to effectively win elections, he relished the conflict. He developed a reputation for being willing to cultivate enemies across the left, his twin targets a Democratic establishment whose approach to campaigning he concluded had grown sclerotic and an ascendant activist corps willfully oblivious to the ways the backlash it generated could be undermining its own aims. But even the benefits of such ruthlessness had limits: the reputational cost of the Alabama scandals was too much to bear.

Within days Mehlhorn began to flesh out a new standard. "Some tactics are beyond the pale," he wrote in Investing in US's annual report. "None of the portfolio we recommended should have engaged in group disparagement or scale misinformation. Such tactics may win a battle but lose the war, by giving up on the American ideal that we seek. We wholeheartedly renounce those tactics and would view it as a violation of our ideals if our resources were used in such ways."

Such a policy would have no official effect beyond the Investing in US portfolio, and perhaps not even be binding within it. But in publicly drawing ethical and moral lines around certain approaches, Mehlhorn had indirectly set a standard that any organization that welcomed significant support from Hoffman—including the committees dedicated to electing Democrats to Congress and governorships—now knew they might be expected to uphold. Entrepreneurs, researchers, and operatives understood what it meant for their work. Early in the American left's reckoning with disinformation, some tactics were already off-limits.

Are You Going to Ignore It?

The first instruction that Jiore Craig gave the new members of her digital team was to begin setting up fake accounts. They started on Facebook, with profiles that were not quite fake. Staffers used their middle names instead of their given names, real selfies in which their faces were obscured, picking their home states instead of the District of Columbia as their current location. They populated the profiles with anodyne content, posting non-political memes and photos of home-cooked dinners.

Then they started asking to join closed Facebook groups with names like Constitution Crusaders, American Patriot Voice, and Telling the Truth About Abortion, which often have "membership questions" that moderators use when determining whom to grant access. (Pro tip: when asked for your favorite year in American history, say 1776.) The team was divided by geography, and staffers sought out state-specific groups covering their areas or related to issues like immigration or land rights of particular local interest there. (Any user could search names and descriptions of closed groups on Facebook and then apply to join them, while private groups are accessible by invitation only and entirely invisible to non-members.) There was no automated way to monitor what was being discussed in such closed spaces; to do so required an ethnographic approach with a hint of subterfuge. "It's all manual," says Craig, "but, you know, it's intern-level work."

Facebook automatically suggested other pages to follow. The recommendation algorithms were opaque, and there was no way to know to how much it was shaped by the user's own behavior, but there were clear indications that they were at least in part informed by the page's attributes—likely directing users to other pages with which one shared followers. All these connections went into spreadsheets, where programming software could render it as a network, providing the first sketch of the information environment in a given area. Once a specific client came along, Craig's analysts would search specific words, phrases, names, and hashtags on the social-media monitoring service Meltwater, which had a full inventory of everything that happened on Twitter and Reddit. They took note of which accounts and platforms were typically effective at amplifying and disseminating content, and researched which were likely bots or trolls.

Craig's team of interns spent much of their days scrolling those groups, looking for stuff they might otherwise try to ignore. When they found something, they pasted the link into their spreadsheets, following the content back to its origins and searching for when it jumped from private groups to public pages or from one platform to another. Then data from Meltwater would help illuminate how information coursed through the network they had mapped.

72   Digital strategists feasted on a constantly refilled buffet of what they liked to call "metrics" in a political sphere that had spent decades painstakingly scrounging enough data to differentiate individual voters. Offline political behavior had been reduced to just one measurable act every two or four years, casting a ballot whose contents remained secret, from which data analysts were forced to extrapolate based on that person's other known characteristics. Social-media data, in many respects, was the opposite. Nearly every online behavior was measured: every click, opened email, site visited, and piece of content shared. But a relatively small portion of that data was reliably traceable back to individuals, which made it often impossible to determine anything about real-world impact—like whether users liking a politician's post lived in her district, or even country. Nevertheless, the natural inclination was to see in this surfeit of metrics a proxy for public-opinion data, made faster and cheaper to collect. To use it one had to accept a series of bold conjectures, such as that people shared content because they agreed with it, for example, or that the candidate with the most online followers should be expected to win.

Social-listening data from providers like Meltwater could be useful to a campaign's decision-making, Craig believed, only if it could be read against a proper context. The first thing her team produced for a new client was a "landscape analysis" that could provide a baseline against which to judge later movement. Did all those Twitter mentions of fluoride in the water supply represent an ascendant concern of voters or just an indestructible myth circulating at the same level it always had? Were they coming from the same cluster of accounts that always promoted fluoridation conspiracies or was the topic winning interest among those typically focused on other issues?

Craig viewed the landscape analysis as the equivalent of a baseline survey that a campaign typically commissions from a pollster at the outset of a race. A campaign that prepared for traditional attacks would typically assess the candidate's shortcomings through research and then use polls to establish which would be the most potent electoral vulnerabilities. A threat assessment Craig supplied a new client would alert him what to be ready for, where to look for it, and when to think it might be a real problem. Only then could a campaign begin to contemplate the full range of potential responses. "The best thing campaign practitioners can really do is they need to have a plan," she says. "But it's similar to insurance—if your insurance policy is working, you don't notice it, right?"

Angus King joined the Senate's Select Committee on Intelligence upon being elected to the chamber from Maine in 2012. Four years later, he met in a Senate office building with a delegation from the Baltic countries, where he pressed his guests on how they defended themselves against Russian interference in their elections. "The most interesting thing they said," King liked to recall, "was, universally, the best defense is for the people to know it's happening."

That became a guiding principle for King after evidence emerged of Russian involvement in the US presidential election. He played a central role in the committee's bipartisan investigation of the matter, which concluded that Russian "operatives used targeted advertisements, intentionally falsified news

74   articles, self-generated content, and social media platform tools
to interact with and attempt to deceive tens of millions of social
media users in the United States." When Congress ordered up a
national strategy for disinformation defense, King was one of
four legislators to grab a seat on the federal commission formed
to draft recommendations. He rarely passed up a chance to
alarm the public about what he knew from classified sources but
could not fully detail. "There is a massive, sophisticated, persistent campaign on multiple fronts to misinform, divide, and
ultimately manipulate the American people," King said in one
committee hearing. "It's more sophisticated than it was in 2016.
They're learning to hide their tracks, not paid in rubles. I would
have thought they would have figured that out before."

Around this time, media consultant Will Robinson, a
part-time Maine resident, approached King on a flight home
to tell him about bot networks he had observed targeting the
senator, and after landing in Portland the two men ended up
at the airport Burger King (no relation) looking together at the
evidence. As King prepared to seek reelection for the first time
in 2018, he grew particularly concerned about the deceptions
known as "deepfakes," which, as King told Facebook COO Sheryl
Sandberg at a Senate hearing, describes the "ability to manipulate video to the point where it basically conveys a reality
that isn't real." They were the year's newest fad in disinformation panic—"Will 'Deepfakes' Disrupt the Midterm Election?"
asked a *Wired* headline—and King scheduled a campaign stop
at a Lewiston digital-marketing agency to draw attention to
the way they could be used to convincingly impersonate politicians' speech. "For somebody in my line of work," King said,
"it's pretty damn unsettling."

King was an Independent, and even though he allied with the Democratic caucus in the Senate, his campaign did not operate with the full backing of the national party committees that had begun offering other candidates general support on matters like protecting their networks from intruders. Campaign leadership attempted to "replicate a classified environment," in the words of digital director Lisa Kaplan, compartmentalizing information on a need-to-know basis, so that a digital intruder who, for example, had penetrated a field organizer's email would not be able to use that to gain access to the campaign's fundraising records. The campaign revived dormant email accounts used by past interns and lowered the security barriers so as to make them appealing targets for hackers, then filled the inboxes with fake strategy memos and polls and invented office gossip. The objective was to "create confusion about what emails are real versus intentionally planted should an adversary attempt to use the information against you or leak emails to the press," as Kaplan put it.

At Robinson's urging, King hired Greenberg Quinlan Rosner to advise on disinformation strategy, eventually paying a total of just over $25,000 for its work. After producing a landscape and threat assessment, Craig led trainings with campaign leadership and staff on topics like "smart social listening to digital metrics that matter" and "comparing online conversation to wider public opinion." The campaign's digital team reoriented itself around the new threat; at one point, among its twelve interns, just four were working on traditional content creation and implementation while eight were dealing with disinformation.

In September, a video began to circulate on Twitter purportedly showing King slurring his words at a campaign stop.

76   His campaign had already taken one basic step to defend against such incidents by being unusually vigilant about ensuring that every one of King's public appearances was committed to video. Now they could unearth a shot from a different perspective that clearly demonstrated the one online had been slowed down, and that could be provided to Twitter in an attempt to have the original posts removed from the service, which represented the most basic, low-cost response available to a campaign. (A few months later, a similarly manipulated video featuring House Speaker Nancy Pelosi, typically with comments suggesting she was drunk, was spread widely across social media.)

It was a far more primitive editing job than the deepfake technology about which King had been warning, and there was no evidence of a more sophisticated plot than perhaps one right-wing Mainer trying to humiliate his elected representative. But nevertheless a frisson of excitement ran through King's headquarters when the video surfaced—the threat the campaign had prepared for was finally here. "This Russia stuff is fun. You know, 'Oh, we found this, we think it's Russian!' And you talk about it and everyone gets upset about it," says Robinson. "A lot of Jiore's time was spent telling us to stop worrying about what's happening. Worry about what you're going to do about it. Are you going to ignore it? Are you going to answer it? Or are you going to do something else?"

The next month, King's name appeared on an 8kun bulletin board dedicated to QAnon research. On the day that Brett Kavanaugh was sworn in as a Supreme Court justice, an anonymous user posted an alphabetical roster of Democrats who had voted against his nomination, with King squarely in the middle. "We need memes and info to meme on everyone listed here," the user wrote, either promisingly or ominously depending on how damaging one thought memes could be. One King staffer inclined toward the latter view insisted that the campaign had to push back. "There was absolutely no need to do anything about it. We didn't have evidence that it reached anybody. Engaging with it absolutely would have given it more traction," says Craig. "Because it had originated from the internet, people don't know how to use their normal brains."

To help explain decisions that for her were generally intuitive, Craig plotted a matrix grid with nine cells, pitting the likelihood a campaign was being targeted by disinformation against the likelihood that the incident would cause votes to be lost. In the corner where both probabilities were low, the guidance was to "do nothing." The opposite corner, where both were high, was full of recommendations: "platform takedown request, change the subject, attack messenger, outreach to voters, press statement or earned media play, run paid campaign, deploy digital organizers or field, response from allies or influences or media coverage." The cells in the middle, which campaign staff might find themselves exploring if unable to make a confident assessment, were filled with passive half-measures like "monitor for escalation" and "arm organizers with talking points."

Craig had found herself in an unusual position. She was becoming a consultant whom clients paid to tell them what not to do. Her job was to get a campaign to the point where it could confidently agree, and stick with it against the natural impulse to do something, anything, in the face of an attack.

King won reelection by a large margin, and shortly afterward Craig's attention turned back to Europe. After being fired from

Trump's White House, Steve Bannon relocated to Italy and attempted to organize a continent-wide right-populist faction he named The Movement. "They see what Breitbart did and they want it in their own language," Bannon told *The New York Times*. He located a medieval monastery south of Rome and vowed to convert it into a "gladiator school for culture warriors" whom he would teach the "fundamental building blocks for winning" the next spring's elections for European Parliament.

American progressives tended to view this new development with a mix of bemused curiosity and distant alarm. But Craig sprang into action, flying back and forth to Paris on her own money to rally a digital opposition to Bannon and his new allies. It was, primarily, a logistical exercise. European countries imposed more restrictive campaign-finance laws, including bans on employing foreign consultants. Craig's project coordinated local survey and focus-group research across the twenty-four languages of the European Union, paired it with social-media monitoring being done by think tanks and academics, and then developed a framework to legally share findings and recommendations so that campaigns and parties running in each of the member countries could make decisions about how and when to respond.

After a year and a half working primarily in Washington, Craig was eager to use the lull after the 2018 midterms to get back onto the international scene, especially at "this rare moment where twenty-seven countries are about to have an election all at once." But she also understood that domestic donors with their eyes on 2020 would value the opportunity to study Bannon's methods so as to be better prepared when they were marshaled again to win the American presidency. (Bannon's movement effectively collapsed beforehand, although like-minded parties made gains in the election and reorganized themselves as a new parliamentary group afterward, and his falling-out with Trump turned out to be temporary.)

"She is constantly power-mapping how to create the incentive environment for the person to say the things that they should say," says Tara McGowan, the Democratic digital strategist, who in 2019 became Craig's roommate in Washington. "She's very smart at understanding psychology and thinking about how to get people to do what you want."

On July 25, some of the left's largest donors—notably those affiliated with the Democracy Alliance founded by George Soros—came together to establish a new entity named the Strategic Victory Fund. As a nonprofit organization, its money could not flow to partisan candidates for office, but in "trying to focus donors on state-level races rather than just national politics," as executive director Scott Anderson explained, it had electoral impact in mind. Over the course of the year, the fund would raise $43 million, and later it created a sister super PACs that spent an additional $14 million in 2020 with fewer restrictions. "The Strategic Victory Fund (SVF) is a community of donors that prides itself on being innovative, strategic, forward-thinking, and collaborative; we are incubators, we scale capacity, we invest in states, and we are committed to progress," the organization reported to the Internal Revenue Service on its activities, including "a major initiative to build a highly functioning and integrated system to track, investigate, and respond to public disinformation."

That initiative brought in experts with a range of experiences confronting disinformation, including some who had been

80   previously focused overseas. "I didn't take my global work off
until fall of 2019, when it was clear that there was enough political will to do something on disinfo here," says Kristina Wilfore,
an American who was based in Istanbul and working in Belarus
when the fund launched. They looked in particular for groups
that did not typically specialize in counter-disinformation but
whose existing work could be made valuable to the mission.
They identified a voter hotline already run by Common Cause
that, if linked to digital-monitoring efforts could prove mutu-
ally beneficial—Common Cause might understand some of the
more outlandish complaints and queries registered by callers,
while generating new leads for researchers to pursue online. The
literary nonprofit PEN America received a grant to produce a
media-literacy program it called Knowing the News.

For the most important part of the well-funded new collaborative, donors had to lean on the Democratic National
Committee along with the party's congressional and gubernatorial campaign arms to participate. The relevant model was a
Democratic Data Exchange unveiled that February after years
of contentious negotiations. The arrangement moved control of
the party's voter database to an outside, nominally for-profit
entity that would be funded with unlimited private, undisclosed
dollars. (Democrats also had to contend with an initiative from
former Obama White House technologist Mikey Dickerson,
with backing from Reid Hoffman's Investing in US, to create its
own rival voter database.) Party committees and independent
groups forbidden from coordinating directly could swap intelligence on the voters through the new entity as long as economic
value was attached to each data transfer. Much as it had been
for Republicans when they created a similarly structured Data

Trust after 2012, it took a presidential defeat for state parties and interest groups to overcome their reluctance toward sharing data they had collected.

A disinformation-tracking consortium could similarly avoid redundancy and disperse costs by charging Democratic party committees, state parties, interest groups, and super PACs for subscriptions to the research it produced. Party organizations could freely distribute the research to candidates of all levels, and offer a central point of contact with the tech platforms when campaigns needed to raise an issue with something moving online. Craig was told she was the only person with the background to get the novel structure off the ground, even though to her frustration it reified the existing separation between those who determined how politicians proactively communicated online and those who trawled the internet in search of potential harm. She knew accepting the assignment would get her personally farther from some of what she liked most from her overseas missions: working alongside candidates to hone a message. "I didn't want to be only monitoring, only listening, only finding the bad. I wanted to be explicitly connected into an offensive arm," says Craig. "Eventually, the pressures were too strong and I said yes."

She rushed to hire twelve more employees to her digital team at Greenberg Quinlan Rosner, seeking out those with personal familiarity with the political environments they would be asked to document. She went on LinkedIn and searched for a Spanish-speaking opposition researcher in Texas. She hunted for those with proficiency in Asian languages. She offered the barista from her favorite Washington coffee shop a job when she learned the recently graduated English major was from

82   Pennsylvania. "I would rather hire someone who had experience working than someone with a graduate degree," says Craig. "That gives me a better sign that they will be able to understand an average voter."

They produced documents covering nineteen states, including both battlegrounds and those like New York and Illinois that would not be competitive but where influential conservative media and advocacy organizations were based. Others concerned Trump and the debate over his impeachment, and a variety of issues popular among conservative voices online: abortion, immigration, right-to-work, voter fraud, Islam. A few covered disinformation targeting specific racial and ethnic minorities. Craig began drafting threat assessments for each area, and her analysts compiled Excel spreadsheets with the names of accounts, keywords, and phrases that campaigns should monitor themselves.

No one could agree on what to call the new structure, and it did not quite matter since participants were discouraged from acknowledging its existence. "We didn't have a name, we don't talk about it publicly," says Wilfore. "It was behind the scenes, feeding information to progressive organizations in order to help prepare them for actually dealing with the firefight of disinfo."

Eat the Babies

Shortly after voting to pass a bill to protect student-loan borrowers from damage to their credit scores, sixteen Democratic members of Congress headed three blocks south of the Capitol and ducked out of the frigid winter night into a borrowed townhouse where a fireplace smoldered as a chef toiled in the kitchen. None of those who had received an invitation knew quite what to expect from the evening. "I've convened this dinner tonight because I think we all know disinformation is not going away," Illinois Representative Cheri Bustos told them.

Bustos was a popular figure among her peers. She had first been elected to Congress in 2012, from an agricultural and industrial district that hugs the Mississippi River, and after a 2016 landslide reelection, the same year her constituents voted for Donald Trump, Bustos became a model of how Democrats could compete in adverse environments. Before the 2018 election, she was appointed to lead the Democratic Congressional Campaign Committee's "heartland engagement" efforts in rural

84   Republican-held districts. After helping her party take back
the House that year, Bustos was elected by the new majority to
lead the campaign committee through an election cycle when it
would have to defend forty-four so-called frontline incumbents
likely to face serious challenges. She decided to hold a monthly
midweek dinner series to tell her fellow House Democrats what
her priorities were, devoting the first to disinformation. "I hope
you will all just quickly talk about why you are here tonight,"
she directed her guests once they had taken seats around a long
table.

There was Suzan DelBene, a former Microsoft executive
who made technology policy one of her top legislative priorities. There were members of the House Intelligence Committee,
which as part of its investigation into "Russian active measures" had released a full list of accounts identified by Twitter
as part of suspected bot networks run by the Internet Research
Agency, and an archive of 3,500 different Facebook advertisements purchased by the agency along with all the targeting data
demonstrating how clearly the goal was to divide Americans on
existing racial, ethnic, gender, and political lines.

Then there were others, like Debbie Mucarsel-Powell, who
had come to this issue purely as a matter of self-preservation.
Mucarsel-Powell had begun to detect a swirl of Spanish-language
disinformation moving through her Miami district, jumping
from local talk-radio stations to paid newspaper inserts to private WhatsApp groups. Over a two-hour conversation, some
of the attendees found themselves on the verge of tears as they
recalled receiving threats so credible they had begun to retain
private security to protect themselves, their spouses, and their
children.

Also at the table that night were two young committee staffers previously unknown to most of the elected representatives. Bustos introduced them as leaders of her new Disinformation Task Force, who could speak in greater technical detail about their work—a gentle way of distinguishing the clear emotional suffering that disinformation caused from its potential electoral harm.

"I took every single one of those seriously and then I let our experts figure out exactly what we needed to do," says Bustos. "Is this a serious disinformation effort against this member or against this campaign—or is it something where we could just maybe soothe some feelings?"

Bustos's interest in the disinformation problem had been triggered the previous spring, when she began hearing from other members about increasingly odd questions they were receiving at town-hall meetings. In one particularly baroque example, a woman in Queens introduced herself as a supporter of freshman representative Alexandria Ocasio-Cortez, who shared her fear about the effects of rising carbon-dioxide emissions on the climate. "We don't have enough time!" the woman exclaimed. "We need to eat the babies!" A political action committee associated with gadfly conspiracist Lyndon LaRouche took credit for staging the encounter—"sometimes, only satire works," it explained—but that did not stop prominent right-wing voices from distributing a video clip without any of that essential context. Tucker Carlson aired it on his Fox News show, as supposed evidence of Ocasio-Cortez's extreme environmentalism, and Trump shared it on Twitter with the annotation, "AOC is a Wack Job!"

When colleagues relayed these experiences to her, Bustos would respond with a story from her first campaign for Congress in 2012. A former journalist, she developed a habit of reading deep into the reader comments on local-news stories about city government, often to her frustration. One night, her husband saw Bustos scrolling angrily and asked why she persisted in doing so; it was not making her any better at her job, he said, and reminded her she had employees paid to ensure she saw anything that would. It had been eight years since she last read an online comment, Bustos said proudly, like a recovering addict measuring days of sobriety. The message she wanted candidates to take away from that story was that they did not need to waste time worrying about this stuff. "We've got your back," she liked to say.

But when the first reports started coming in from town-hall meetings, committee officials did not quite know even how to categorize the problem. Field organizers were asked to look into how event attendees had been recruited while regional political directors worked directly with candidates to prepare them for events. But it quickly became clear the issue was fundamentally a digital one. "We asked them where they heard that, where they saw it, and it was the same answer across the board," says online rapid-response director Ben Block. "'Facebook.'"

Block's job was a new one. After graduating from college, he had worked for a young consulting firm, Mothership Strategies, which became known for a relentless approach to email fundraising that critics called "churn and burn." He then went to the DCCC as its email production manager and spent 2018 managing one of the nation's most active email lists, testing the effectiveness of messages against one another and ensuring they evaded spam filters. Over the course of the year, Democrats raised over $100 million online, but Block grew cynical about the methods that made it possible. Online fundraising was often too desperate, too coercive, was disrespectful of the party's most loyal supporters in a way that no politician would countenance if done offline. He wanted to do something different.

Block pitched his bosses on creating a new digital department that would do more than solicit supporters for fundraising and volunteer tasks; it would not simply rely on paid advertising to persuade non-supporters. Traditionally "rapid response" had been a job for a press-secretary type who worked only reactively and spent his or her days interacting with reporters to shape news coverage. But Block argued for using the DCCC's large online footprint, including two million followers on Facebook, to get its message out. "We weren't doing much to move any of those conversations or to engage in them," he says. The Democratic party committees that came together to form the new disinformation federation differed widely in how they decided to use its output. The Democratic National Committee would look out for the party's presidential candidates, both during the nominating season and general election, and help state parties that wanted to prepare their own defenses. The Senate and gubernatorial campaign arms would supply their candidates with monitoring reports from Greenberg Quinlan Rosner, but trust them to build internal digital and communications teams that could manage a response. The congressional committee would treat disinformation monitoring much as it did other fundamental campaign functions, from drafting opposition-research binders to profiling voters. "I don't know of any campaigns where they had people on their staff who addressed this," says Bustos.

Bustos put Block in charge of the DCCC's new Disinformation Task Force, and he assigned one of his rapid-response team's five members, who had been working on content creation, to spend half his time on the initiative. "We understood this was clearly a problem and our campaigns were not sufficiently prepared to combat disinformation attacks. But let's figure out what's causing this problem and how it functions," he says. As part of its contract with the counter-disinformation federation, Greenberg Quinlan Rosner supplied unique landscape analyses and threat assessments for nearly three dozen districts, and then began tracking the content moving across them. Block's team set up a "secure incident tracking system" to take in complaints from candidates and a "rapid response service bureau" to guide them through potential responses within Craig's matrix, helping explain the logic of "do nothing." But Block knew his team would be uniquely valuable in situations where a threat landed in the corner that included the recommendation of "platform takedown request."

For years, technology companies had expanded their presence in the capital, aiming to build and deepen relationships across the partisan divide. Facebook made the biggest impression, spending $81 million between 2010 and 2019, when—as an indication of intention of future growth—it opened an office with space for 200 employees. They interacted with officeholders in nearly every capacity. A corporate political action committee handed out contributions to candidates. Company grants went to think tanks and interest groups, from conservative advocacy organizations to minority business associations, to shape the conversation on Capitol Hill across a range

of issues. On the most urgent of them, lobbyists attempted to
persuade lawmakers to the company's side, largely to fend off
new regulations or at least to shape them so they would do more
harm to competitors.

While the public-policy team exerted pressure on chiefs
of staff and legislative aides, the politics-and-government-
outreach team was offering to help press secretaries and digital directors in congressional offices make better use of their
accounts for reaching constituents. At the same time, sales-
people were pitching the lawmakers' campaigns and the party
committees to budget more money for advertising on company
platforms. The largest spenders were assigned full-time dedicated Facebook staffers. Many of those staffers had previously
worked as partisan digital operatives, for whom there was little obvious difference between encouraging candidates to spend
online and advising them tactically on how to win.

Now the politicians would have to use those relationships to
get the companies to take their disinformation complaints seriously. The party operative who best understood how to do that
was Tim Durigan, who had worked on the DCCC analytics team
in 2018 and the following year became the Democratic National
Committee's first staffer dedicated to counter-disinformation.
One of his first projects was a systematic effort to compare the
platforms' policies for what could be published. Some forbade
certain types of threats and harassment, while others prohibited
nudity and sexually explicit material. Others policed imperson-
ation or misrepresentation. Most tried to keep out spam and
bots. There were different penalties for violators, from warnings to takedowns of specific posts to lifetime bans from the

90   service. Some companies held candidates and elected officials
to a different standard than civilians, in the interest of news-
worthiness. Twitter restricted political ads altogether.

Many of the platforms attempted to enforce these policies through technical solutions, typically algorithms that
could detect inappropriate material like nudity or racial slurs
and automatically remove posts that included them. These policies relied on fine distinctions that were constantly subject to
change—Facebook at one point exempted mastectomy photos from its nudity category after pressure from breast-cancer
awareness advocates—but nevertheless computers could be
trained to learn them. (The platforms typically had appeal processes available to users who believed their content had been
mistakenly identified by the system.)

But there were no predetermined rules about what qualified
as misinformation. An assertion could be false one day and true
the next, or accurate coming from one speaker but inaccurate
from another. Developing the capacity to make those judgments
quickly would require significant investments in manpower,
and would open companies up to second-guessing about the
subjective assessments they made. For years, Facebook said it
would not ban misinformation, but merely adjust its algorithms
to reduce the rate at which it spread, so as to make it less likely
to appear in others' news feeds—a strategy whose implemen-
tation was conveniently difficult for outsiders to assess. "The
question is," Facebook operations specialist Henry Silverman
wrote, "how do we come up with a model where we're serving
people by giving them a chance to see the content they want,
while also cutting down on misinformation, without having
Facebook be the judge of what is true?"

No major social-media platform had a policy of removing
misinformation about political or social issues, but Facebook
had gradually imposed limits on other categories of speech.
After deadly incidents of religiously and ethnically targeted
violence in Sri Lanka, India, and Myanmar inspired partly by
online rumors, Facebook announced in the summer of 2018 it
would begin deleting misinformation created "with the purpose
of contributing to or exacerbating violence or physical harm."
Then, with an eye to the upcoming US midterm elections, the
company added factually inaccurate material related to the process of voting to the list of immediate takedown targets.

In November, one year ahead of the 2020 presidential election, the company unveiled an altogether new approach to "fake
news." Facebook would now designate media organizations as
fact-checkers, and rely on their rulings to label posts on any
topic as inaccurate, including through pop-up windows that
warned users they were about to share a post with "false information." But still Facebook would not entirely stop or remove
political misinformation—"Share anyway" was a pop-up
option. "Part of our work to stop the spread of misinformation
is helping people spot it for themselves," a corporate blog post
explained.

Durigan, who had become an expert not only on the changing standards but also on the peculiarities of each site's processes, became the primary point of contact with the platforms.
He worked first to cultivate ties at Google, Facebook, Twitter,
and Snapchat, the ephemeral short-video site that had begun
to win serious attention as a political-communications tool
during the midterm elections. Any user could report inappropriate content within a platform, which placed it in a queue

92   for review by content moderators. When something required immediate attention, Durigan often sent an email to the public-policy teams, who could intervene to prioritize a particular item—and were motivated to keep politicians happy. (Although Twitter appeared to insulate the "integrity" team that enforced platform policies from the company's lobbyists, it became clear that Facebook's Washington office was empowered to make decisions about content on the site.)

As the election year went on, urgency on such requests would likely grow, and it was useful to begin early moving items through those channels. "Open the door and start getting things actioned," Craig advises. "That just establishes you as a trusted flagger worth knowing." To do so required not only learning the specifics of each platform's policies, but developing a lawyer's instinct for appealing to the authority for getting them enforced. Durigan had learned the value of first bringing straightforward cases to build credibility, like those in which an account impersonated a candidate or used clearly pornographic imagery, which would indicate to the politically minded employees that they were helping to enforce the platforms' rules rather than challenging them.

Even as their staffers worked to navigate the platforms' processes in private, politicians were coming to see the political benefit of letting such conflict also play out in public. Despite their historical reliance on Silicon Valley for fundraising, Democrats found its most prominent consumer-facing companies to be appealing targets for the types of populist attacks they had previously aimed at oil drillers and pharmaceutical manufacturers.

That February, a week after the townhouse dinner, Trump shared a video that spliced together two separate episodes from C-SPAN's coverage of his State of the Union address two days earlier. First he was shown paying tribute to Charles McGee, a decorated Tuskegee Airman who had attended the speech as one of Trump's guests. Images of McGee were interspersed with those of House Speaker Nancy Pelosi, seated behind the president, contemptuously tearing up the text of his speech. There was no indication that any images in the five-minute video were distorted, merely juxtaposed in a way that left the impression they occurred concurrently—"Powerful American Stories Ripped to Shreds by Nancy Pelosi," as the video's text explained.

"The American people know that the President has no qualms about lying to them—but it is a shame to see Twitter and Facebook, sources of news for millions, do the same," Pelosi's deputy chief of staff Drew Hammill wrote on Twitter, whose headquarters happened to be in Pelosi's San Francisco district. "The latest fake video of Speaker Pelosi is deliberately designed to mislead and lie to the American people, and every day that these platforms refuse to take it down is another reminder that they care more about their shareholders' interests than the public's interests."

The video did not, however, appear to violate policies on "manipulated media" that either platform had begun to implement. (These policies were partly a response to alarmist warnings from media and politicians about deepfakes, which had retained a centrality in press coverage of disinformation threats even as they were scarce to materialize in the real world.) Two days before Trump shared the Pelosi

94   video, Twitter had issued a new policy singling out "significantly and deceptively altered or fabricated" audio and video "shared in a deceptive manner." (Violations would be marked with a warning unless it was determined that they could cause harm, like violence or "widespread civil unrest," in which case the post would be removed entirely.) Facebook had recently released its own policy that applied only to videos reshaped by artificial-intelligence or machine-learning tools "in ways that are not apparent to an average person, and would likely mislead an average person to believe that a subject of the video said words that they did not say."

A Washington-based Facebook spokesman who had previously worked for congressional Democrats, including at the DCCC, responded directly to Hammill's post. "Sorry," wrote Andy Stone, "are you suggesting the President didn't make those remarks and the Speaker didn't rip the speech?"

"What planet are you living on? this is deceptively altered. take [sic] it down," Hammill answered.

Within the DCCC's Disinformation Task Force, the exchange was an early indication of how things were likely to play out in practice. Tech companies might adopt new anti-disinformation policies, and Democratic operatives could master them. But the companies were not going to be willing partners in enforcing their own rules as aggressively as Democrats would like, especially if the required action would appear to be taking sides between partisan antagonists in an election season. When one of them occupied a position of power, and was already the biggest single political spender on Facebook, companies would look for any reason not to act. "This

is an industry known for spinning stories and persuading voters," Block says of campaigns. "The platforms will often push
back and say 'Well, that's not exactly disinformation.' What
they're not always willing to do is look at the motives behind the
message."

On April 15, 2020, Craig stared into a web camera and began to
teach Democratic members of Congress about online disinformation. Her team had mapped the online landscape in many of
their districts, part of a mad scramble for the federation to finish the first stage of its research by the arbitrary deadline after
which campaigns and outside groups were forbidden from coordinating their efforts. Any materials completed before that
point could be freely shared, allowing the entire American left
to work for the duration of the election off a shared understanding of the threats it faced. After the deadline, Craig had had to
cut off communication with the so-called soft money independent groups and interact only with partisan organizations that
were subject to strict campaign-finance regulations.

Craig had expected to spend much of the year traveling from
one campaign office or state-party headquarters to the next,
delivering versions of the same training to those on the front-
lines against potential attacks. But the arrival of the coronavirus pandemic changed that. Most campaigns suspended all
in-person activity; the DCCC would, controversially, keep the
prohibition in place for the rest of the year, both as a practical
matter to protect volunteers and voters and also as a symbolic
gesture to communicate that the party took the public-health
crisis seriously.

A few weeks earlier, the DCCC had promoted the creation of its Disinformation Task Force to the media, an unusually bold commitment to work that other organizations were working to keep private. There were many risks to being so public, such as drawing special attention from trolls eager to provoke a response, or setting the committee up for claims of hypocrisy if any of its candidates made false claims. "We wanted the outside world to know that we had a way to combat the disinformation that was out there," says Bustos. "If you're gonna mess with us, we've got a way to come at it."

Craig's team had begun producing regular reports for Block's team on noteworthy content moving across the online landscapes in nearly three dozen of the districts of those in attendance. "The DCCC already has a sophisticated disinformation operation," she explained, "but the nature of the problem makes it nearly impossible for any one organization or tool to detect and manage all potential threats."

Craig knew that, as federal legislators, those in her audience were not altogether new to the topic. Sitting members of Congress and their Capitol Hill staffs likely thought about disinformation foremost as a national-security problem or a public-policy matter, just one element in a debate over regulation of big tech taking place within both parties. (In perhaps the boldest move of her brief presidential campaign, then-senator Kamala Harris had demanded that Twitter suspend Trump's account for violating its anti-bullying policy, and then struggled in vain to get rivals to join her.) Craig implored her audience to realize the "unique partisan objective" needed to guide their response as candidates, and that they could not count on tech

companies—even those that regularly approached them with
the blandishments of lobbyists—to act with any urgency at a
moment of concern.

Craig itemized some "common campaign pitfalls" that
stemmed from such misunderstandings. Campaigns decide
impulsively to respond, take a reactive posture of fact-checking
and overexplaining that helps to amplify the original material. In so doing they drive media coverage that focuses on the
"sides" disputing the truth, losing focus of the voters whose
opinions should remain a campaign's priority.

When she had made similar presentations to DCCC staff,
Craig had focused on the short-term threats that she said
required "day to day firefighting," like manipulated media
related to breaking news or dishonest statements from Trump,
and storylines that had to be tracked over weeks or months,
like disinformation over the state of the economy or directing
blame for the pandemic. But to lawmakers she also emphasized
threats presenting long-term peril, like online misinformation
deployed to foster further racial division, distrust in media, or
denial of climate change. "Everyone we were talking to should
care about one of the things on those slides," says Craig. "We
were trying to make the point that it was worth the investment."

That winter, events were helping to make the point to members of Congress, too. All but four House Democrats voted
to impeach Trump for exerting pressure on newly elected
Ukrainian President Volodymyr Zelensky to investigate former
Vice President Joe Biden's son Hunter's work for the Ukrainian
oil company Burisma. No longer content to launch falsehoods
about his opponents from his own Twitter account, or to rely on

98   rapid supporters to propagate their own, Trump had attempted
      to wield the powers of the White House to make a disinforma-
      tion narrative real. He had been acquitted after a Senate trial,
      and he vowed to make his reelection a vengeance tour. The
      potential emergence of misinformation was no longer a tactical
      subplot to an election that would be decided on other factors,
      but increasingly a central element in the plot itself.

The Malarkey Factory

On August 31, 2019, at 3:17 p.m., two Texas state troopers driving on a frontage road along I-20 in Midland attempted to pull over a gold Toyota sedan for failing to signal. The driver did not stop, and instead began shooting an assault-style rifle through the car's back window, hitting one trooper in the face as his partner returned fire with a handgun. The Toyota sped away westbound on I-20, its driver calling 911 and taunting operators as he unloaded his rifle into other cars around him, exiting the highway once he reached Odessa. There he spotted a postal worker sitting in a delivery van, grabbed her arm, shot her in the head, and took her vehicle. He continued through Odessa, shooting other motorists while heading toward a crowded movie theater where police had established a roadblock. He crashed the van, and, after a brief firefight with officers, was killed, about an hour after the chase had begun. Crime scenes stretched across ten miles and multiple jurisdictions; it took hours for authorities to conclude that he had acted alone. The next day, at noon, the Odessa Police Department held a press conference, and shortly thereafter identified the suspect in the deaths of seven and injury of twenty-two others: Seth Aaron Ator, a thirty-six-year-old recently fired from his job at an Odessa oilfield. His motive was unknown.

Within minutes, a Twitter user named @suem054 posted a message on the platform that read, "The Odessa Shooter's name is Seth Ator, a Democrat Socialist who had a Beto sticker on his truck." This was entirely baseless: neither vehicle that Ator drove had any political markings and he showed no sign of affiliation with any political movement. (Ator was registered to vote but like all Texans did so without partisan affiliation.) Almost instantaneously the post was retweeted hundreds of times, despite the fact that @suem054—whose previous tweets had been largely links to Facebook posts—had only 364 followers. Soon other Twitter users were posting the same false claim using identical language, and also finding their tweets amplified beyond what would be expected from the organic reach of their followings. By 6:00 p.m., a majority of posts across Twitter mentioning Ator also included "beto" and "democratic socialist" (or a variation). Overnight the claim jumped to Facebook, where users would supply supposed documentation: an image of a white truck affixed with a "Beto 2020" decal. (The image was taken from the Etsy page of a store selling campaign stickers.)

On the morning of September 2, the presidential campaign of former Texas congressman Beto O'Rourke heard from the Democratic National Committee's counter-disinformation intelligence unit. The DNC had earlier hired its first full-time counter-disinformation staffer, Tim Durigan, who became a linchpin of the new information-sharing network within what it called the "Democratic ecosystem." The DNC gave all the candidates the same counter-disinformation training and collected guidance in a newsletter that went out to all. It would be the responsibility of campaigns to decide how they would use the knowledge provided to them.

The campaigns had wildly different ideas about what action was appropriate. Massachusetts Senator Elizabeth Warren, who said as president she would enact "civil and criminal penalties for knowingly disseminating false information" about voting, took the most proactive approach. She launched a "Fact Squad" page on her website so comprehensive that it surfaced allegations receiving little traction elsewhere: "No, Elizabeth Warren Does Not Have a Racist Artifact in Her Kitchen" and "No, Elizabeth Does Not Take Risperdal," a drug used to treat schizophrenia. Others were more passive. When the National Rifle Association's television channel aired a segment claiming that Vermont Senator Bernie Sanders supported giving terrorists the right to vote, based on posts from a Twitter account impersonating Sanders, it was not his campaign but the magazine *Mother Jones* that brought the issue to Twitter's attention (and had the account taken down).

Only upon detecting an urgent threat uniquely targeting one candidate would Durigan offer a campaign a specific warning, as was the case when he alerted O'Rourke's digital director Rob Flaherty to what he had been seeing related to the Odessa-Midland shooting. The way the lie had spread so widely—it was mentioned in 12,856 tweets from 11,566 accounts within the first twenty-four hours after Ator was named, according to one disinformation analyst, through quick spikes without promotion by any major accounts—was a telltale sign of a bot network at work. Researchers at Media Matters identified a number of the accounts that spread the Odessa rumor as also having played a role promoting the QAnon conspiracy theory.

At O'Rourke's El Paso headquarters, the DNC alert was welcome but unaccompanied by much useful direction. O'Rourke's communications staff encouraged mainstream media to write about the hoax, noting that advisers to Donald Trump's reelection campaign had helped disseminate it and accusing social-media platforms of deciding to "refuse to act on this because they're afraid of the political consequences," as campaign manager Jen O'Malley Dillon told the Associated Press. That may have advanced O'Rourke's strategy of standing out in a large primary field—there was no better way to elevate oneself above rivals than to pick a fight with Trump— but also drew attention to a story otherwise stuck in an online cul-de-sac. "As a campaign, we're almost entirely powerless to stop misinformation," O'Malley Dillon lamented on Twitter. "We can tweet corrections, but only a fragment of the people exposed will see it."

Two months later, O'Rourke would be out of the race, and both O'Malley Dillon and Flaherty would be on their way to the campaign of another Democrat who would feel less powerless in that conflict. "There's value in being more aggressive about this stuff," Flaherty said that October. "Traditional political communications tells you that if there's something in the grocery store tabloid it's not worth talking about it because it just raises it up. The lesson for us is to be confrontational."

In March 2020, days after Joe Biden effectively clinched the Democratic nomination, he hired O'Malley Dillon to manage his general-election campaign, reuniting her with Flaherty, who had already become Biden's digital director. One of her first tasks was to set a budget against an opponent who had been collecting money for his reelection since the day he was sworn in, while Biden had lagged behind in fundraising. In March, when Biden defeated the others and could look ahead to the general election, he had just one-quarter as much cash on hand as Trump, who had been building a national organization for a year. Biden's campaign prepared for a contest in which it would operate at a severe financial disadvantage against the incumbent. But within weeks, Biden's campaign leadership realized their budget projections had been too conservative. In May, Biden for the first time raised more over the course of a month than Trump, and by fall it was the Democrat who was setting records, eventually raising $365 million in August and $383 million in September.

Recognizing that the campaign would likely be flush with cash all the way through Election Day, O'Malley Dillon in mid-summer issued Flaherty an unusual invitation: How would he spend an additional $10 million?

Flaherty thought back to the final line he had jotted in his notebook while serving as deputy digital communications director for Hillary Clinton in 2016. In the closing days of the race, the campaign learned from the social-listening service Bottlenose that it was being targeted by bot networks. Even though Flaherty had been dealing for months with the fallout from the Russian hack-and-dump operations, upon receiving the Bottlenose report he was forced to confront the reality that the campaign had given little thought to a strategic response. Its pollsters had tested negative messages they thought voters might hear from her opponents, with the idea that the results

104   could inform how one campaign responded to another incident. They had heard some of the wilder conspiracy theories in focus groups. But no one had considered misinformation as a distinct form of political speech, requiring its own set of tactics, and certainly no one had actively sought out the wildest examples to measure their potency. In his notebook Flaherty scribbled an instruction to himself, unheeded on the short timetable that remained: *We should talk to the paid advertising team about misinformation.*

Over the next few years, he and Rebecca Rinkevich, a digital ad-buying specialist at Bully Pulpit Interactive, began a rolling conversation about what that might look like. In 2018, when Flaherty was trying to elect Democratic senators as creative director of the Priorities USA super PAC, they experimented with what they called "prospective advertising." Since the 2004 election cycle, candidates had been buying search ads on Google against particular keywords, such as their own names and sometimes their opponents', to draw traffic to their own websites, most typically for fundraising purposes. But as the ability to retarget advertising grew, Flaherty and Rinkevich saw the opportunity to grab a voter at a moment of curiosity and then, essentially, keep badgering her as she traveled across the internet. A person in St. Louis who in the fall of 2018 searched for material about a centerpiece of the QAnon conspiracy theory might be shown a display ad that read "Sex Trafficking in Missouri? Josh Hawley thinks women are responsible for it." (The Republican Senate nominee had blamed the sexual revolution and other cultural changes for the rise in trafficking.) Clicking on the ad sent the user to one of several issue-specific anti-Hawley landing

pages, from which a browser cookie could ensure that when the
St. Louisan next went to watch a video on YouTube, she would
first sit through an ad about the Senate race.

Two years later they were in a very different position.
Flaherty dedicated the new digital budget to what some took to
calling the Malarkey Factory, after an old-timey Bidenism that
had already been appropriated as a secondary campaign slogan; that winter, a desperate Biden undertook a No Malarkey
bus tour across Iowa before that state's caucus. The new investments would include online organizing efforts to stitch together
progressive-minded accounts that could be activated to disseminate coordinated messages from the campaign. One initiative solicited homemade recordings from swing-state voters
testifying to their support for Biden, tested their effectiveness
against one another on online survey platforms, and then delivered them to voters whom statistical models identified as most
likely to be persuaded by them. "He came to me with a couple
of things that we had talked about over time if we were able to
design programs to take it on. One of those things was disinformation," says Rinkevich. "Once the money was on the table, we
actually put pen to paper."

The centerpiece of the project was a program that would
isolate the type of disinformation that could prove to be
"market-moving," in Flaherty's preferred phrase. "My theory of
what a campaign can do came down entirely to, 'We need to figure out whether or not this is actually affecting voters or just
inflaming the right,'" he says. "Is it destabilizing or demobilizing
our base? Is it persuading voters? And if it's not, it is a problem
for society. But it's not a fifty-plus-one problem."

Rinkevich took the assignment back to her former firm. Bully Pulpit had emerged from Obama's 2008 campaign to become the dominant digital ad buyer in Democratic politics. Since then, the firm had built a public-opinion research team, which included Jessica Reis, who had worked for Greenberg Quinlan Rosner's international team for thirteen years, across Thailand, Serbia, and South Africa. "After dealing with 'foreign' political issues like extreme polarization, Russian meddling, disinformation, uneven media environments, 2016 happened, and I looked up and said, 'Wait a minute, I've seen this before,'" she says. "And that spurred me to get more involved in US domestic campaigns."

Where digital strategists might be inclined to see each claim as a discrete piece of information, public-opinion researchers instinctively looked for the ways in which they were linked in the minds of people who were receptive to them. "Voters made sense of these narratives in ways that social media algorithms would not," wrote Bully Pulpit partner Danny Franklin. "Identifying the connecting point between disparate narratives let us calibrate our response."

He and Reis drafted a survey based on the monitoring data and analysis that her former teammates at Greenberg Quinlan Rosner were funneling to Biden's campaign through the Democratic National Committee on a daily basis. They isolated the prominent misinformation narratives related to Biden's candidacy, covering a wide range of topics. Often the best shorthand for each came from Trump's own epithets: Biden staffers lumped some together as "Sleepy Joe" (related to Biden's age and mental fitness) and others as "Creepy Joe"

(QAnon-inflected tropes about him being sexually predatory toward younger women). Others related to Hunter Biden's business dealings and personal life. Some concerned Biden's newly selected running mate, California Senator Kamala Harris. A few anticipated attacks that would have likely been deployed against any Democratic nominee, such as the claims of "socialism," used with particular effect among Spanish-speaking communities in Florida, where voters associated the term with left-wing regimes in Cuba, Venezuela, and Nicaragua. Reis and Franklin also seeded the list with a few calumnies they themselves had conjured, like the baseless and heretofore unaired charge that Biden had been a member of an all-white country club, and dubbed them "red herrings." This fake fake news could act as a baseline for comparison with the claims that had been circulating online.

The disinformation narratives were presented through an online survey, so voters would see the claim on a screen instead of having it read to them, an attempt to mimic how an individual would be most likely to encounter such material in the wild. There were three questions about each narrative. The first: *Regardless of whether you believe it or not, have you seen or heard anything about this?* The second: *Do you believe it is mostly true?* It was the third question that was most important in determining the shape of the threat: *Does that raise doubts for you about voting for Joe Biden?*

Responses were plotted on a grid, where the horizontal axis measured voter awareness of a particular claim and the vertical axis the projected impact on vote choice. This harm index would help determine the campaign's response. "By focusing on the impact, rather than the source or the volume, we developed a response strategy designed for persuasion," Franklin wrote in a memo. The left-hand side of the chart represented low danger. Anything on the right required "close watch," since it stood to be damaging if it caught on further. Anything that landed in the upper-right quadrant, where voters were both aware of a claim and indicated it could change their opinions, demanded swift action.

Bully Pulpit would conduct their polls on a weekly basis, allowing Reis and Franklin to adjust the position of narratives on the harm index, to add new ones that the federation's monitoring picked up, and to permit the campaign to test various responses. "Working in these environments a lot, you think you get a sense of what's going to have impact and what's not going to have impact," says Rinkevich. "There were some real surprises."

"We all know about Joe's son Hunter Biden," former Florida attorney general Pam Bondi said in her speech to the Republican National Convention on August 25. It would be hard for any American to have avoided learning something about the ne'er-do-well who had won a lucrative seat on the board of the Ukrainian energy company Burisma, without any evident experience or expertise, while his father served in the White House. The story had fascinated conservative media ever since Biden had expressed his intent to seek the presidency in 2020, and the quest to unearth some sort of corrupt bargain beneath it—in which American interests were subverted for the Biden family's private gain—drove Trump's first impeachment. After he was acquitted by the Senate, two Republican committee chairmen pursued their own investigation of the Bidens' ties to

Burisma. "The more that we expose of the corruption," one of
them, Wisconsin Senator Ron Johnson, asserted that summer,
"would certainly help Donald Trump win reelection and certainly be pretty good, I would say, evidence about not voting for
Vice President Biden."

When the polling data came back, it became clear that while
many Americans did know about Hunter Biden, few of those
surveyed seemed to take it very seriously. (An interim report
from the Senate committees, released that October, would offer
no evidence that American policy changed as a result of Hunter
Biden's involvement in Ukraine.) While 66 percent of voters were aware of the Burisma story, only 38 percent said that
it would affect their vote. It sat at 25 on the harm index. When
that month the contents of a laptop belonging to the younger
Biden became public, his father's campaign pushed Twitter and
Facebook to suppress posts derived from it, claiming that they
violated company policies about nudity and hacked material—
as some cybersecurity and law-enforcement figures then suspected but subsequent reporting has shown to be false—but
still did not worry about it as an electoral problem.

By contrast, the Sleepy Joe narrative had not only reach but
potential to damage. Eighty-three percent of those questioned
were aware of the questions about Biden's mental fitness, and 40
percent said that those questions had generated questions about
voting for him. When plotted on the harm index, Sleepy Joe sat
near a seemingly unrelated narrative that Harris was a "far-left
radical," as one Trump campaign press release put it, a theme
that circulated in right-leaning Facebook pages and groups at
a high pitch over the summer as she became the obvious front-
runner in the vice-presidential selection process. When Reis

and Franklin dug into the poll data, they realized that proximity was not coincidence. Many of the people who expressed concern about Harris's ideology were also anxious about Biden's age and acuity. (A somewhat competing narrative, that Harris had been too aggressive as a local prosecutor—"Kamala is a cop," in the shorthand of progressive activists—worried only college-educated white women, who said it would not affect their support for Biden.)

When Reis hosted focus groups, the link between the two became evident. It was an unwritten rule that in their exploration of disinformation, the Biden campaign and its consultants did not want to be in the position of spreading it themselves, so Reis fell back on a technique she had practiced when questioning voters in Serbia and Venezuela. Where typically a focus-group moderator might try to keep an overbearing participant in check, for fear that his kooky musings might derail a discussion, Reis had a strategy to put him to service. (The pandemic-era shift from in-person meetings to videoconferences made excision of a troublesome guest easy; the moderator could simply press a button and innocently blame inexplicable tech problems if other participants took note of their shrinking number.) Reis would ask her guests what was the wildest thing about her candidate they had encountered. After something was mentioned, Reis would ask others if they had heard it, too, often opening the vein of conjecture, conspiracy theory, and falsehoods that she wanted to hear but could not elicit directly.

When Reis replicated this for Biden's campaign, she very quickly realized how futile it had been to press a voter about whether he or she believed a given narrative was "mostly true," as the polls asked. "It's not whether you believe it to be true or

not," says Reis. "If it's having an impact on your vote, that's the
thing that matters. If it makes you doubt voting for him, then
you believe it."

Rather, she saw how the narratives fit into voters' world-
views regardless of how they assessed the relative truth or falsity of each specific claim. The messaging most damaging to
Biden shared a common foundation, an underlying anxiety that
he was a weak leader who would not be fully in control of his
government if elected. The focus on Harris's record was not
simply about the vice-presidential nominee's qualifications,
but the concern that she would serve as a shadow president, and
maybe even ascend to the office herself before Biden's term was
up. It was in those same groups that an explanation of the surprising weakness of the Burisma attacks emerged: persuadable
voters generally did not see Biden as motivated by self-interest.

These insights laid a basis for the campaign to respond,
its goal less debunking falsehoods than generating counter-
narratives to address the deeper doubts. Focus groups had
revealed that the voters the campaign would be trying to reach
were skeptical of its messaging and would likely resist conventional advertising pushes or anything that appeared too deliberately packaged. "Unless a new piece of information is surprising
in some way, voters will sort it into their preexisting narrative
or dismiss as a falsehood," Franklin concluded. "To change a
narrative, both the source and content of the information need
to be somehow jarring."

Biden's communications advisers had assumed that the
best way to rebut the Sleepy Joe attacks was to make sure voters saw him at his most physically vigorous, like jogging along
parade routes or bicycling for exercise. But the weekly polls,

112   enriched by perspective from focus groups, pointed toward more basic fixes. Voters responded positively to clips of Biden speaking clearly and authoritatively about his values, directly at the camera without obvious edits, and to unlikely validators attesting to his robustness: a Fox News article about law-enforcement officials endorsing Biden, a *Wall Street Journal* op-ed from a retired Navy admiral headlined "BIDEN WILL MAKE AMERICA LEAD AGAIN." "It wasn't so much that the goal was to show him strong physically, but we had to show him strong standing up for himself, standing up for those Scranton values, not being controlled by those fringe elements that people are worried about," says Franklin. "That was the thing, rather than running up the stairs, that made people feel like he was going to be the author of his presidency."

Flaherty's team aimed its response across Google's network so the ads appeared on pages including keywords tied to the disinformation narratives (like "Kamala + cop" or "Biden + senile," for example). In so doing, the campaign turned what Flaherty called the "problematic inventory" into a practical vector for showing a counter-message at exactly the moment when people were being exposed to the disinformation. Someone reading an October newspaper article about a Trump campaign press call featuring Ronny Jackson, a former White House doctor turned Republican congressional candidate, was likely to see the Biden campaign's response in the form of what must have appeared to be a non sequitur: a lightly edited thirty-second debate clip in which the former vice president references his working-class childhood in Pennsylvania and Delaware to empathize with a contemporary family's anxieties about being able to afford replacement car tires.

The research team liked to say this approach reflected the principle of approaching the problem from the demand side rather than the supply side. "It's tempting to see the spread of disinformation as a problem born of social media. While there's no question social media accelerates the spread of disinformation, narrowing one's focus to the platforms misses the scale and nature of the problem and distracts one from the solution," Franklin wrote in a post-election memo to the campaign. "The channels through which disinformation flows do not matter so much as a subject's willingness to believe it and the decisions they take as a result."

In that memo, Franklin celebrated the program but indicated one key note of caution for those who might see it as a template for every future effort to combat lies online. "The power of anti-Biden narratives was limited by Trump's reputation for dishonesty," he wrote. "Any story Trump elevated carried with it a shadow of doubt. Without his toxic brand as a marker, voters in the middle may see disinformation as more credible."

Believers
by Default

The creative brief that David Goldstein drafted in July 2022 was the type of thing that regularly fell into the boxes of political consultants who made a living producing television and radio spots, online display ads, and direct-mail flyers. The four-page document cited qualitative research to describe the target audience and laid out five intended messaging tracks for changing its beliefs, suggesting possible themes and language. "We seek to understand what styles, tones, and visual cues within digital creative can successfully pull a section of Big Lie believers away from this dangerous false narrative," Goldstein wrote. "Understanding the different approaches that digital creative can take toward increasing confidence in our election system maximizes our ability to inoculate current and potential voters against disinformation surrounding it and the election process."

But when Goldstein finally hit send, his primary audience was not a media consultant or direct-mail vendor. Rather it was someone who had tallied more than one billion online views by matching brief pop-culture snippets with absurdist and often

self-referential dialogue, and whom for years his new patron
had known only by a pseudonym that did not necessarily fore-
tell an interest in helping to solve a global epistemological crisis.
"The single most effective communicator in the digital space I
had ever seen," says Goldstein, "was this guy named IH8MyPP."

Behind the IH8MyPP screen name was Beau Elliot, who in the
spring of 2015 saw a colleague laughing in the break room of the
English-language school in Istanbul where they both taught.
The colleague introduced Elliot to a website called Imgur, an
image-hosting service that had become a gallery of very online
humor. Elliot set up his own account, basing his user name on
something he affectionately recalled his then-teenaged daughter saying as a toddler when he told her to use the bathroom
before bed. Elliot, who had once tried stand-up comedy as a
hobby, took to the visual, largely silent medium—one fit for
quiet browsing on public transit. Over the next few months,
he posted images to both Imgur and Reddit, incorporating
Rodney Dangerfield punchlines, a shapely Mexican meteorolo-
gist standing in front of a green screen in an inadvertently racy
way, and the kumru, an epically unhealthy Turkish sandwich
"loaded with what Dr. Kevorkian called, 'The Cure!'" as Elliot
wrote in the caption. "It was just something entertaining," he
says. "Imgur gave me a platform where I was able to create stuff
and come up with some jokes and make people laugh."

Soon Elliot was spending more than eight hours a day teaching himself graphic-design and photo-editing software, taking advantage of the difference in time zones to post his newest
work in the morning when American online traffic was high. As
he grew more skilled, Elliot moved away from the static images

116   and started experimenting with video, which, he came to appre-
ciate, allowed him to stuff more jokes into each piece of content.
On August 14, IH8MyPP published an "unpopular opinion puf-
fin" meme that declared, "I'm not that fond of memes anymore."

Elliot's new chosen genre was the gif, a short-form file format typically configured to automatically play in an endless
loop without any prompting. (He pronounces it with a hard
"g," as in "girl.") Where most of the gifmakers he knew began
with a piece of found video, removed the sound, and then created new captions that matched up with the action, Elliot usually approached his work the other way around. He did so the
way a *New Yorker* cartoonist might, coming up with a joke or
comical scenario and then ransacking his vast memory of often
unexceptional television and movies for an appropriate visual
backdrop. The IH8MyPP trademark was to render speech captions not as film-style subtitles but as a form of dynamic text
that contorted a speaker's body as almost an extension of the
character, the words following people as they moved, occasionally casting shadows or showing their reflection in a mirror. His
subject matter varied—"some jokes are a little edgier than others; some [are] just cheesy dad jokes," he says of his oeuvre—
but in the finest metapoetic tradition, many concerned the act
of gifmaking and the peculiar online cultures that surrounded
them.

In December 2016, Elliot produced the gif that would
make IH8MyPP famous. He grabbed thirty-five seconds from
a trailer to the film *Guardians of the Galaxy Vol. 2,* and reshaped
its dialogue into an exchange about the peculiar mores of posting on Reddit bulletin boards. "Guardians of the Front Page"

was for years the platform's most popular post, upvoted nearly
300,000 times; on Imgur it received over 140 million views. In a
comment thread, fans exchanged theories about its exceptional
popularity. "It's funny, about Reddit, is quality, and it has nothing to do with American politics," one user wrote in an effort to
explain the video's immediate popularity. "It's the right gif at
the right time."

Among IH8MyPP's fans was Goldstein, who browsed Imgur
to satisfy both an ongoing curiosity about new communications platforms and a dark, occasionally joyless sense of humor.
(He describes visiting the site not for laughs but "little sero-
tonin hits.") He did not learn the gifmaker's real name until
Elliot entered a contest to become Bud Light's "chief meme officer" and began rallying his online fans to vote for him. Goldstein
contacted Elliot, who had since moved back to the United
States, settling in Oregon as he tried to assemble enough free-
lance assignments to devote himself full time to making digital
content. "Would you ever be interested in doing political work?"
Goldstein asked over video chat.

Goldstein had spent his career at political polling and digital marketing firms, but following 2016 he started to question
many of the assumptions that had guided their approaches to
communication. "The thing Trump and Brexit have taught me
is *worry about engagement first, persuasion later*," he says. "A terri-
ble problem on the left today is we're worried about messaging
before we even worry about whether or not people are going to
hear the message." To test whether pro-Trump "methods could
be replicated and improved upon in an ethical, legal, yet still
effective manner," Goldstein started a firm called Tovo Labs,

borrowing its name from the word for "hope" in Finnish. "If any-one had caused problems for the Russians, it was the Finnish," he says.

In 2017, Tovo Labs raised $100,000 in independent-expenditure funds for a pilot program during the special election to fill Alabama's vacant Senate seat. "We basically ran what we consider to be a Trump-style campaign, which is essentially aggressive, really eye-popping digitally," says Goldstein. He identified two sets of three similar state senate districts that could be paired under experimental conditions, and within them he targeted moderate and conservative Republicans with two different digital ad campaigns. The graphics were garishly crude, like something a color-blind person might have made on second-generation desktop-publishing software, with links to similarly amateurish websites filled with text from articles written elsewhere. The conservatives were shown prominent evangelical religious figures criticizing Republican nominee Roy Moore. The moderates were introduced to Republicans planning to write in another option on their special-election ballot, such as Luther Strange, the establishment-minded incumbent whom Moore had defeated in the primary.

It was a lot like the "voter suppression" campaigns that Trump advisers had boasted about in 2016, but Goldstein could point to evidence that his project had been successful. After the election, he measured a decrease in turnout among the moderate Republicans targeted with ads in the treated districts of 2.5 percent, and 4.4 percent among the conservatives, compared to the control districts. (The total number of write-in votes state-wide exceeded Doug Jones's margin of victory over Moore, with

about one-third of them going to Strange.) "In sum," Goldstein
wrote in a post-election analysis, "we believe strongly that the
results of this experiment indicate that the left can reap sub-
stantial gains from taking an aggressive stance with integrated
digital innovation."

He spread word of his findings to prospective donors quietly
until journalists investigating the two Investing in US-funded
false-flag operations came across the project Tovo Labs had been
simultaneously running. Goldstein courted media attention
but nonetheless found his work often lumped together with the
other Alabama campaigns as Democratic disinformation offen-
sives. (A flattering National Public Radio segment was titled
"How to Meddle in an Election," over Goldstein's half-hearted
protest.) He struggled to find progressive campaign organizations willing to give his tactics a shot; even MediaMath, the
ad-buying platform Tovo had used to target Alabama voters,
was wary of being identified with the firm's future efforts. "It's
aggressive, and that scares people. They thought it was just in a
gray-enough legal area, and they were worried about bad PR," he
says. "The blowback against guys like Reid Hoffman was enor-
mous and was chilling." Goldstein spent much of 2019 sick,
from an ongoing heart condition, and by early 2020 was ready to
give up on his hope of finding a sponsor.

Then he met Jehmu Greene, a self-described "evange-
list for good and a serial political entrepreneur" who had led
Rock the Vote and the immigration reform organization Define
American. But her pivotal experience may have been the
decade she spent working for the Fox News Channel. The network's founder, former Republican campaign operative Roger

Ailes, had become an unlikely mentor. "I was intimately famil-iar with his reputation and the products he created, and at the same time very comfortable with knowing who I am, what I believe in, and what I fight for," says Greene. "And he wanted to amplify my voice." In 2010, Greene was offered a contract as a Fox News analyst, a liberal African American woman put in the often thankless position of defending the Democratic posi-tion on the network's shows. When she briefly took a leave in 2017 to run for the Democratic National Committee chairman-ship, she claimed that experience as a credential. "As someone that has spent the last six and a half years on Fox News, debat-ing, and fighting with conservatives that don't know anything other than to lie for a living," Greene liked to say, "I've been able to win with the truth." Greene helped convince Goldstein that they should work together to defeat Trump's reelec-tion with some of the same coarse tactics and aesthetics that had helped launch him into the presidency in the first place. Along with a third cofounder, tech entrepreneur Matt Mireles, in the summer of 2020 they launched an organization called TruthNotLies and set out to make an impact that November. (It was structured under a section of the tax code that imposed no limits on contributions and required minimal public disclo-sure while forbidding "express advocacy" for or against a spe-cific candidate.)

The goal was again to test "persuasion with a group that is almost completely ignored by traditional progressive election-eering," as a post-election report put it. Goldstein had analysts isolate 1.4 million Pennsylvania voters whom statistical models pegged as Trump voters in 2016 but likely to be uncertain about their 2020 choice, and divided them into control and treatment groups. (Pennsylvania was chosen over other top battleground states due to its proximity to New York and Washington, which Greene and Goldstein thought made it more likely to draw press coverage.) TruthNotLies would approach them as they had Alabamians: they presented every reason not to cast a ballot for their Republican nominee without explicitly discouraging anyone from voting.

After the election, a poll conducted by the firm PredictWise would measure whether voters in the treatment group saw their opinions diverge from those in the control group. Until then, Goldstein would rely on a constant cycle of experimentation, known as A/B testing, to refine the content most effective at driving voters to websites where the persuasive material resided. But Goldstein wanted to feed a wider range of visuals than just the intentionally ordinary static images of flags and crosses he had used in Alabama. "I knew what I had done in 2017 was not going to cut it in 2020," he says. "It's always progressively harder to break through." He looked to forms indigenous to the internet.

Goldstein approached one producer whose distinctive video style was interspersing shots of himself with movie footage, a graphic designer who manipulated photos to create arresting new images, and a former MTV reality-show editor with a knack for squeezing drama out of short passages. IH8MyPP's work had only occasionally, and glancingly, touched on current events, and Goldstein worried that like many online mischief-makers his politics would lean right, or at least in the direction of MAGA nihilism. Instead, when asked if he would accept commissions for political work, Elliot set one condition: yes, as long as it was not for Trump.

Within weeks, TruthNotLies ads began appearing across Facebook and Instagram and sites like Breitbart and Fox News. Almost immediately, it became clear that nearly all the best-performing content came from Elliot. (They lacked their creator's name or pseudonym but bore his distinctive style.) One gif, titled "Trump's Stump," reimagined a scene from *The 40-Year-Old Virgin* in which the main characters look through a "big box of porn" to remind viewers that Trump had paid off an adult-film star to remain silent about their affair. Another had characters from *The Office* puzzling over his penchant for saying "I wish her well" when asked about Ghislaine Maxwell following her arrest in the Jeffrey Epstein sex-trafficking case. Another pulled from the straight-to-DVD 2007 comedy *Big Stan,* for a gag in which a new inmate given a prison-yard tour is warned to steer clear of the toughest gang, introduced as "Trump's campaign associates and advisers."

The ads were shared more than 550 times, which Goldstein considered "a stunning result, as it is typically impossible to get your opponents' supporters to share negative content about your opponent." Between 1 and 2 percent of those shown the ads clicked through to a pair of intentionally underdesigned websites, named Truth Yum and Truth Crusaders, where TruthNotLies warehoused more substantive anti-Trump content. After the election, polls found voters shown the ads moved away from Trump and toward Joe Biden by several percentage points, which PredictWise calculated was responsible for generating a total of 20,000 net Democratic votes.

TruthNotLies had spent only $146,000, and after the election the group's most significant donor, New York venture capitalist Albert Wenger, said he thought he would have had much greater success raising money if soliciting tax-exempt charitable gifts rather than political contributions. Goldstein and Greene, after an acrimonious split with their cofounder Mireles, reestablished the organization under a new name. As a nonprofit, it could not advocate for one candidate or against another, but could run advertisements educating the public on particular issues. They could aim, they wrote in a strategy memo, to "disrupt damaging, hurtful narratives by serving content many right-wing voters never encounter from individuals, media, and organizations that they admire (e.g., military voices, religious leaders) and doesn't trigger their mental defenses and create backlash."

For much of 2020, Goldstein had toyed with launching a campaign to confront one nonpartisan delusion that had spread throughout the country: a lack of confidence in coronavirus vaccines. At the start of the next year, events presented him and Greene with another. We Defend Truth would try to use the same tactics they had—coarse, ugly, funny, unexpected, occasionally vulgar—to try to push voters away from disinformation itself.

Starting almost immediately after Election Day, some of the most prominent Republicans in the country—beginning with the president—asserted that Biden had won only because of fraud. They offered a grab bag of conjecture for what might have happened, from suitcases of ballots magically appearing from under desks to something about Italian satellites changing tallies on electronic voting machines. Every theory was rejected by courts and regulators across the six states where Trump and his allies contested his narrow defeat. (Trump lost sixty-one of sixty-two post-election lawsuits, and three statewide recounts did not materially change his position.)

On January 5, the first damage of Trump's two-month-long campaign against what he called a "rigged election" revealed itself in the form of political self-harm. In Georgia, voters faced a runoff election for both of the state's two Senate seats, after no candidates had won majorities in November. Trump only half-heartedly campaigned for his party's nominees in the run-off, using rallies in the state to complain about the legitimacy of Biden's narrow victory there rather than promote their cause. When on January 5 Trump's party found itself swept out in a state that prior to his presidency had been reliably Republican for a generation, it became an article of faith among Republicans critical of Trump that his assertions of a corrupt voting process had been a crucial factor. "He told them their votes didn't count, and some of them listened," said Scott Jennings, an adviser to Republican Senate leader Mitch McConnell, who lost his majority. "Telling everyone that the race was stolen when it wasn't cost the Republicans two Senate seats," said Erick Erickson, a Georgia-based blogger and radio host. (Trump himself later conceded the causal link without acknowledging his role. "They didn't want to vote, because they knew they got screwed in the presidential election," he told journalist David Drucker.)

The next day, a mob of Trump supporters—inspired by the same lies said to have kept Georgia Republicans from the polls and egged on that morning by the president himself—invaded the United States Capitol in an effort to halt the certification of Biden's election. Lawmakers fled the building as intruders ransacked offices and smashed historic furniture; seven people, including three police officers defending the Capitol, died as a result of the hours-long siege. It was the closest the country had come to democratic collapse since the Civil War.

Goldstein followed the attack on the Capitol via radio as he drove his kids around New York, warning them, "The one thing we don't want to start hearing is gunfire." When it came time to reimagine their organization with a nonpartisan agenda, he and Greene decided to take on the deception that had led Americans to turn against the institutions of their own government.

The relaunched We Defend Truth made a priority of unwinding what was dubbed "the Big Lie," the unfounded claim that Biden orchestrated a conspiracy to rig the election. The name derived from the insight of Nazi propagandists that big lies could be more persuasive than small ones. "It would never come into their heads to fabricate colossal untruths, and they would not believe that others could have the impudence to distort the truth so infamously," Adolf Hitler wrote in *Mein Kampf.*

Once Goldstein and Greene set out to raise money from liberal donors, they found many who saw their quest as well-intentioned but grandiose and counterproductive. "There were a lot of people who not only thought we were being stupid, but were questioning our sanity," he says. "They were like, 'Why do you want the other side to feel better about our elections? The entire reason we grabbed two seats in Georgia and took the Senate was because these idiots didn't come out to vote because they thought it was all fraudulent.'" Aiming funny gifs at the type of people who just launched a violent insurrection was a fraught and potentially hazardous exercise. ("It would've required the same kind of caution, security, craft that goes into

126   countering ISIS and others online," Goldstein says. "Felt a bit
       beyond our remit!") But, he believed, if they could separate such
       dead-enders from those just beginning to entertain the con-
       spiracy theory, there might be a role for We Defend Truth to
       play, disabusing the latter group.

       To perform that triage, We Defend Truth hired FrameShift,
       which had been founded by consumer-marketing veterans
       whose application of unconventional techniques made them
       almost instantly popular with progressive operatives and
       donors seeking fresh approaches for winning back voters who
       had turned toward Trump. We Defend Truth asked the firm to
       generate a psychological profile of Trump supporters who could
       be moved "away from false information regarding fraud in our
       elections and toward stronger confidence in the integrity of our
       electoral system (and thus the work of our election officials)."

       Researchers recruited sixteen people, diverse in race, gen-
       der, and geography, united in having voted for Trump in 2020
       and now expressing at least some doubts about the legiti-
       macy of Biden's victory. Over a ninety-minute Zoom session,
       these subjects were asked to generate a "fantasy story about
       your trust being restored in public systems, including the elec-
       tion process," and then to use Google search to identify images
       that would illustrate that story. FrameShift then assembled
       the images into a sort of collage that it described in marketing
       materials as "like a police sketch of your subconscious."

       Juan, a twenty-three-year-old Latino man, produced an
       image that had gloomy clouds ("because there's no trust")
       yielding to clear skies, where a man with an I VOTED sticker in
       his hand ("holding it up happily because it finally got counted")

basks in the sun. In one corner there is a cup with a hole in its bottom since, as Juan told his interviewer, "certain people know they're filling it for no reason, others don't." In the middle of the image, however, spotlights illuminate a scoreboard with a red team vs. blue team tally. "As soon as I vote, I can see that my vote made a difference," explained Juan. "The conspiracy about our votes not counting completely goes away."

FrameShift divided those it studied into three subsets. There were Strong Big Lie Believers, who believed Biden definitely did not win the election, and Big Lie Believers, who had some doubts about the legitimacy of his victory. Juan fit in a third group, Believers by Default, who had a tentative relationship to the conspiracy theory, being unsure about it, or accepting or rejecting it only weakly. A FrameShift survey found that they comprised 30 percent of Trump supporters questioning the election's legitimacy.

The survey also revealed some promising avenues of approach for We Defend Truth. Believers by Default were not conspiracy theorists and had never sought information about the Big Lie; it had come to them, fed by suspicions related to the days it took to determine the 2020 winner in many states. Now 91 percent expressed some degree of concern about fraud in the upcoming 2022 elections, but it appeared to derive from a good-faith belief that the system that oversaw voting was complicated, vast, and a little chaotic. "These people still have trust in a lot of the institutions, which for us was a shock. I never even would have asked that in a survey, because I want to just assume that all of Trump's people think our institutions are shitty," says Goldstein. "But these folks seem patriotic, such that, you know, things like American democracy is something that we're proud of. And so there was a clear line of attack that we knew we needed to take—tapping into the pride and patriotism."

Goldstein's creative brief characterized Believers by Default as "a hopeful group, mourning divisions in society while desiring to see people compromise and meet in the middle." It laid out five different creative tracks, each appealing to a different aspect of this worldview. What America Does Best would appeal to patriotic pride in American democracy. Demystify Voting would highlight the existing safeguards that make large-scale fraud nearly impossible. Value of Questioning Things would encourage curious viewers to redirect the skepticism that opened them to the conspiracy theories back onto the theories themselves. Rule of Law would frame election denial as undermining the criminal-justice system. Harmony would present an appealing vision of moving on from the conflict around 2020.

Elliot was the only creator whom Goldstein entrusted with the assignment, and the direction provided was to create gifs on each theme that would prioritize amusement over persuasion. "From my perspective, you earn the right to be able to share your message with your audience. And you earn that by doing something for them, entertaining them, validating their identity," he says. "You know the bullshit you always hear about how an attention span is 3.2 seconds long? Well, then, how do they read thousands of pages by J. K. Rowling? If you engage with something, the attention span goes up exponentially."

Within days, Elliot had returned a gif for each creative track, for which he was paid about $400 each. All were relatively faithful to the source material, with Elliot remixing the dialogue to address current events, each with a different tone. Rule of Law featured a speech from Sacha Baron Cohen's *The Dictator* so as to liken the film's fictional North African autocracy to the contemporary United States. For the What America Does Best track, a *Talladega Nights* scene in which two rival race-car drivers argue about the merits of their respective countries redirected the viewer's national chauvinism in such a way that would provoke a viewer's defensiveness about credible elections as part of American culture. Demystify Voting had an exchange from *30 Rock* recast to point out that claims of election fraud seemed to come only from those who had lost, never from those who won. Value of Questioning Things repurposed a string-laced evidence corkboard from *It's Always Sunny in Philadelphia* to illustrate the irony of those who aim their skepticism at official explanations but gullibly accept kooky conspiracy theories without doubt. For the Harmony track, Elliot remixed an inspiring speech from *The American President* to earnestly rally a common bipartisan disdain for "an attack on our democracy," with no actual acknowledgment of the Big Lie itself. (For this, Goldstein hired a voice actor to narrate Elliot's captions.)

FrameShift tested the gifs' effectiveness by randomly assigning them to five thousand people on an online-survey platform to detect which ones caused viewers to change their opinions on questions around voter fraud. The patriotic What America Does Best track was persuasive with Republicans who opposed Trump, but not Believers by Default. None of the other tracks pushed that target audience toward rejecting the Big Lie, either. In fact, two of them were altogether counterproductive. The Rule of Law track left Believers by Default feeling "personally attacked" by the ironic comparison of the United States to a North African dictatorship, according to the FrameShift

130   analysis, while the Value of Questioning Things "reminded people WHY they questioned the 2020 result in the first place (e.g.,
rumors of dead people voting, fake votes across regions) and as a
result, many in our target audience felt validated."

The dismal findings diminished Greene's hopes of using
positive experimental results to raise more money in the final
stretch before the midterm elections. (So as not to run afoul of
Internal Revenue restrictions on political activities by nonprof-
its, the ads would continue to run well beyond Election Day.)
Despite once entertaining grander ambitions to shape voters'
views during an election season in which Republicans nomi-
nated several prominent candidates who promoted the Big Lie,
after spending research and production costs, We Defend Truth
was down to an advertising budget of approximately $300,000.
There were 3.6 million Believers by Default spread across
Pennsylvania, Georgia, and Nevada, all of which featured close
Senate races, competitive contests for their governorships, and
were typically presidential battlegrounds. To save money, We
Defend Truth dropped plans to have FrameShift build a statistical model that would individually identify voters likely to be
Believers by Default. Instead it used an existing microtarget-
ing category that most closely resembled those targets, called
Entrepreneurial Conservatives.

Over the course of the advertising campaign, Elliot's gifs
received a click-through rate between 3 and 4 percent, with the
average user spending just under one minute on Truth Yum or
Truth Crusaders. About 98 percent of user interactions with
the content on the platforms it appeared were positive (likes,
laughs, loves, and shares). We Defend Truth included these in a

summary they would send to prospective donors as they set out to raise money for 2024. Unlike the persuasion experiments, Greene and Goldstein knew these statistics were blessedly free of useful points of comparison: there were not many campaigns that had ever tried to target entertaining content at their opponents with the goal of moving them off their misconceptions.

"The reason why those aren't popular metrics is because most advertising campaigns—corporate or political advocacy of any type—don't really anticipate that the target audience will enjoy their advertising," says Goldstein. "The assumption when we're going so many levels deep on a very pernicious myth is that we can't talk to the misinformed citizenry. What we're trying to say now is not only can we talk to them, not only can we reach them, not only can we persuade them, we can actually make it a fun, enjoyable interaction."

We Defend Truth's first work of 2023 would be a Texas project funded by the Gill Foundation, a Denver-based organization that has been the nation's most important backer of LGBT-related causes. Elliot began working on gifs that would use humor to help undermine anti-transgender disinformation like the surprisingly persistent urban myth that, as Colorado Representative Lauren Boebert repeated it, educators "are putting litter boxes in schools for people who identify as cats." Greene and Goldstein hoped success would, among other things, inspire interest in their tactics ahead of the following year's presidential and congressional elections.

While doing so, they pulled away from their initial promises of being able to correct disinformation, and toward a new, untested theory of how to engage with those who believe

132   lies: "Delighting our audience is fundamental to We Defend Truth's ROI."

"From people who want to address disinformation, there's a lot of funding going to research. There's a lot of funding going to tracking. There's a lot of funding going toward making sure that the regulations that social media companies need to be abiding by are developed, but there's very little funding program work dedicated to the audience that's been misinformed," Greene says. "We still want to do that."

Lawyers, Gifs, and Money

When Brazil's Superior Electoral Court opened a new headquarters in 2011, it represented the most significant new addition the country's planned capital had seen in years. The court is older than Brasilia itself, dating to the 1932 founding of Brazil's system of "electoral justice" at the same time it enacted women's suffrage, the secret ballot, and compulsory voting, which all took effect in the following year's election. "The slave was freed in '88 and the people in '33," Finance Minister Oswaldo Aranha told the newspaper *O Globo* at the time. "These are the two biggest dates of our formation." The authority responsible for administering elections itself moved between unmemorable structures across Rio de Janeiro and then Brasilia once it became the seat of power in 1960, another small federal bureaucracy whose work sustained the nation but rarely drew public attention.

That changed in 2000, when the court replaced paper ballots with electronic voting machines. The technology enfranchised Brazilians who previously lived too remotely to be served by traditional polling places, including in far-flung corners of

134   the Amazon, where it was much easier to tote an individual computer rather than secure cloth sacks filled with paper. More voters saw their preferences recorded, too, as the number of ballots left blank or voided by inappropriate markings fell dramatically. At the same time Americans waited thirty-six days for their presidential election to be settled, a period filled with competing claims of fraud, Brazilians celebrated the bureaucrats who delivered conclusive results within hours. "Our election system has advanced with the passing years," columnist Stephen Kanitz wrote in the newsweekly *Veja*. "Theirs is stuck in the past."

Fifteen years after emerging from a military dictatorship, election administration had become a source of national pride for Brazilians who understood the ways it marked their resurgence into a modern liberal state. "I wish that democracy, so important to us, will continue to be stronger and stronger, taking care of the country's and Latin America's problems," said the architect Oscar Niemeyer, who was tapped to design a new headquarters for the court a half-century after first helping to map Brasilia.

Niemeyer's building was completed in 2011 and now houses nearly a thousand employees who oversee every aspect of the vast nation's electoral apparatus. (Niemeyer died a year after the opening.) But it was not until 2022 that the court's cultural status grew to fully occupy its monumental home, as a faceless custodian of election administration became an active protagonist in a vote the Council on Foreign Relations labeled "a test for democracy."

Over the course of the election year, the Superior Electoral Court became the center of gravity in Brasilia. The presiding judge, Alexandre de Moraes, often showed up in news coverage as frequently as the two leading candidates for the presidency: right-wing incumbent Jair Bolsonaro, pursuing a second four-year term, and Luiz Inácio Lula da Silva, a former president seeking a return to office after spending a year and a half in prison. The court's Portuguese abbreviation, TSE, appeared in headlines as often as the candidates' names. What happened there on a daily basis was much more important to the election than anything transpiring nearby at the city's more enduring icons of political power, the high-rise National Congress or the Planalto Palace, home to the president's office.

Brasilia's jet-age city plan was designed to mimic an aircraft from above, with parts of government assigned to distinct zones based on function: the tail housed the military, the cockpit and fuselage the political bodies, with diplomatic and judicial branches supporting them to the sides. The new accessory in the southeast quadrant disrupted the delicate equilibrium. From one angle, the court's tower looked like a pin used to hold down the right wing and keep the entire thing in balance.

Ten days before the end of Brazil's 2018 presidential election, the nation's leading newspaper, *Folha de São Paulo,* reported that an online marketing firm called Yacows had been hired to blast hundreds of millions of unsolicited pro-Bolsonaro messages to WhatsApp accounts attached to phone numbers acquired from digital agencies. The straightforward scandal was not about the messages' content but their financing. A politician's corporate backers had made prohibited in-kind contributions, which went unreported to authorities, and

136   violated electoral laws permitting digital communication only to supporters who have provided their contact information to candidates.

With time, attention came to focus more on the substance of the messages. Public and private groups on WhatsApp, where according to one poll 57 percent of Brazilians said they received political news, were a gongpit of inaccurate information. The fact-checking institute Agência Lupa, working with two Brazilian academics, collected 100,000 political images from public groups, and analyzed the fifty most shared. The majority, they found, were either demonstrably false, employed misleading context, or made unsubstantiated claims. The most widely shared image of the batch purported to show former president Dilma Rousseff next to Fidel Castro with a caption suggesting she was his "socialist student," even though Rousseff was an eleven-year-old schoolgirl in Belo Horizonte when Castro was photographed with the glam young woman in New York. Only 8 percent of the images were "fully truthful," according to the analysis.

After Bolsonaro's victory, *Época* magazine described how his supporters used WhatsApp to disseminate this material, starting with phone chips sourced from Portugal, Argentina, and the United States and using numbers with country codes attached to India, Pakistan, and Saudi Arabia. Organizers coordinated plans on Telegram, a different messaging application, all presumably to thwart any investigation that might tie the numbers together. A team produced an endless stream of content, from scans of traditional leaflets to original memes, then dispatched it to phone numbers divided by broad demographic segments: evangelicals, women, young people, the poor.

The problem was not limited to WhatsApp, however. One Facebook post alleged that Workers' Party nominee Fernando Haddad, who emerged from the first round to face Bolsonaro in a runoff, had introduced a "gay kit" to schools and day-care centers while serving as São Paulo's governor; an accompanying video showed a baby bottle topped with a plastic nipple shaped like a penis. The original post, which came from the page of a user who elsewhere promoted Bolsonaro's candidacy, may have been intended as satire. Yet that nuance appeared to be lost on many of those who shared or otherwise amplified it, including one of Bolsonaro's sons. By the time the media fact-checking consortium Projeto Comprova investigated the video's claims— determining the nipple was a real item for sale on erotic-toy websites but that there was no evidence anyone had proposed making it available to children—it had already been shared by 71,000 users and viewed 2.4 million times. The original post had been up for two days.

Bolsonaro, who had spent years in the legislature as an irascible backbencher, was known for his hyperbole and infidelity to truth. But this was the first indication of a purposeful effort to use the internet to systematically perpetuate lies on his behalf, so organized that one congresswoman allegedly maintained a calendar of which political opponent to target on each day. Brazilians began to call this enterprise, which was understood to operate from within the Planalto, the "office of hate."

Perhaps most worryingly, Bolsonaro himself questioned the reliability of the electronic-voting system that had never been associated with any indication of fraud since it was first used in 1996. Bolsonaro had criticized the machines since 2014, and had failed in legislative efforts to require a paper receipt of each vote to guard against fraud. (The court determined that such a record would violate the right to a secret ballot.) Even as president, Bolsonaro kept up attacks on the system that had elected him. He claimed to have evidence of fraud but never acted on his promise to reveal it. "We've already made contact with people who understand the subject—they are hackers—to make a public demonstration," Bolsonaro vowed. "Of course the television will not show it, but I will do a livestream."

No part of Brazil's political or media system was prepared to confront the "fake news" problem in the context of a fast-moving campaign. A digital-rights movement that had pushed for passage of a robust data protection law modeled on the European Union's had been built to fight for privacy and freedom of expression, and the disinformation debate was in many respects at odds with those objectives. "When you talk about disinformation, you may be affecting the individual freedom of expression," says João Brant, a communications policy adviser in the culture ministry during Rousseff's term.

The tech companies that were quickly blamed for permitting the "office of hate" to flourish were also blindsided by the scrutiny. In the fall of 2018, Facebook had opened a much-hyped "election war room" in its California headquarters, festooning the walls with American and Brazilian flags in acknowledgment of its priorities. But its subsidiary WhatsApp, which had been acquired by Facebook four years earlier, had considered itself largely immune from many of the same external pressures. WhatsApp had been designed for private one-to-one and small-group messaging, not broadcast or sharing, and did not include advertising within the app. Its executives never had to worry about how to placate commercial interests whose logo might appear alongside dangerous speech and could not imagine ever drawing the attention of regulators. At the time of Bolsonaro's election, WhatsApp did not have a single staffer focused on politics and policy in Latin America.

Brazilian political professionals, too, had given little thought to how they might protect their candidates from harmful disinformation narratives. "We studied Cambridge Analytica, and we studied the Trump process. But when it hit us here, it hit us so fast and so badly," says Gabriel Gallindo, a São Paulo-based media consultant who works for left-wing candidates nationwide. "It's like death. You know it's going to happen, and you prepare. But you're absolutely not prepared, and you only know it when it hits you."

Gallindo had been close enough to the eruption of "fake news" to feel its heat but far enough away to emerge unscarred. During the 2018 election, he advised Guilherme Boulos, a first-time candidate who had led a high-profile movement representing homeless workers, known by its Portuguese abbreviation as the MTST. Boulos made his mark on the election by confronting Bolsonaro at the start of a televised debate, "All of Brazil knows you're male chauvinist, racist, and homophobic!"

It was Gallindo's first political campaign. He had first encountered Boulos in 2010 while a student, and they grew close. Gallindo went on to pursue a career in film, serving as a writer, cinematographer, and director on everything from short-form thrillers and television dramedies to branded animations for IBM and a chef's online cooking series. In 2018, when Boulos accepted the presidential nomination of the also-ran Socialism and Liberty Party, a breakaway faction of the Workers Party,

140   Gallindo enlisted with the campaign team. He was ambiva-
        lent about this move across the amateur-professional divide.
        Gallindo had joined Boulos's movement as an idealistic activist
        who just happened to have skills relevant to political communi-
        cation; he chafed when he now saw himself being characterized
        as a "marketer."

            In his new role, Gallindo had Boulos supporters infiltrate
        private WhatsApp groups where possible, and send reports on
        relevant messages they spotted to campaign leadership. "We
        couldn't even analyze what they're doing, and conclude what
        hurt us the most or what went the furthest," said Gallindo.
        "We didn't have the tools, or they don't even exist." Boulos
        was too insignificant a player in the race to be a focal point of
        many of the disinformation attacks that targeted Haddad,
        Bolsonaro's chief left-wing opponent. (Boulos finished tenth in
        the thirteen-candidate field, earning less than 1 percent of the
        vote.) But there was one storyline that kept surfacing: Boulos
        was preparing to invade your house. Like most successful lies,
        it was not entirely baseless. Starting in 2003, on acres owned
        by Volkswagen, Boulos led efforts to "take over tracts of land
        that are not fulfilling a social function," as he put it, and create
        self-governing communities of squatters—a forcible kibbutz-
        ing of private property that the Brazilian press often described
        as an "invasion." Boulos responded with an earnest rebuttal. "It
        is an absurd invention that the MTST 'invades people's homes,'"
        he wrote on Twitter. "The movement occupies abandoned prop-
        erties, which are illegal or have unpayable debts, which do not
        comply with the law and were not expropriated for social hous-
        ing due to a lack of courage in facing major economic interests."

After his defeat, Boulos made plans to run for mayor of São Paulo, Brazil's largest city, and Gallindo got to work insulating him from a renewal of those attacks. "We're never going to be able to deny with more efficiency and with more amplitude than the fake news, disinformation," he says. "This is a reality—people associate him with home invasion. We can't undo that, that's already done. But what we can do is create another association which is stronger than that. Or we can hack this association that already exists."

The primary channel was a web-video series called *Café com Boulos.* (The title is a pun on *bolo,* a term for cake frequently served alongside coffee.) It was not a natural fit for the fledgling politician; Boulos, a one-time psychoanalyst, had always had a principled disdain for speaking about his personal life instead of policy concerns. In the first episode, he sat at a desk in a bare office and delivered a forty-nine-minute monologue directly to the camera, with only a coffee mug to enliven the tableau. Over time, the production values of *Café com Boulos* improved—graphics, a samba theme song, a set that resembled a home library—and Boulos grew more conversational, developing a comfort, even enthusiasm, with the ritual appeal for viewers to follow his YouTube channel.

One word kept popping up in Boulos's new-style digital content: *invade.* An episode where he made a surprise visit to a supporter's home for coffee was titled, "Boulos Invades Karol's House." Another began with Boulos watching a skit by a prominent comedy troupe, which satirically depicted a "socialist" government social program in which a transgender official forced residents to accept a homeless roommate; Boulos

142   responded with a hearty laugh. During the pandemic, Gallindo
       spun off another video series in which the candidate spoke to
       others remotely, called *Boulos Invades My Home and My Heart.*
       When questioned himself by journalists, Boulos often began
       with a joke about invading their interview. "He uses sarcasm and
       irony, to hack the association that already exists in his regard,"
       explains Gallindo. "It breaks the intention of this negative asso-
       ciation, which is creating fear, and it creates laughter."

       Gallindo's interest, though, was not just to show a softer
       side of the often strident activist or lighten the conversation
       around him. It was also a recognition of the unique economy of
       social media. If anyone chose to push new disinformation (or
       other criticism) on the invasion theme, Boulos would already
       be there. He would have a head start if people searched for the
       phrase on search engines, and for YouTube to queue up when
       its algorithms searched for related videos. If the phrase made
       it onto Twitter or Instagram's lists of trending topics, Boulos's
       own content would get caught up in the riptide, too. Gallindo
       called the technique "clickbaiting their terms."

       Boulos's candidacy for mayor placed Gallindo in the mid-
       dle of 2020's biggest race in Brazil. He did not know how to fight
       disinformation, but he thought he could prepare. "Our job," he
       says, "was to not let it catch."

       In early 2019, Brazil's Supreme Court opened an investigation
       with no evident crime and no known suspect. Chief Justice José
       Antonio Dias Toffoli issued a one-page order citing little more
       than "the existence of fake news, slanderous denunciations,
       threats, and infractions laden with animus *calumniandi, diffa-
       mandi,* and *injuriandi,* which affect the honorability and security

of the Federal Supreme Court, its members, and family members." The court had authority to investigate crimes only when
they took place at its physical location, and given the lack of
specifics, the country's general federal prosecutor demanded
the court explain what crimes exactly it was pursuing. She
got no response, and then called on the court to shut down an
inquiry with no evident legal or constitutional basis. "Complain
at will, criticize at will. Who interprets the Rules of Procedure
of the Supreme Court is the Supreme Court," replied Alexandre
de Moraes, the judge Toffoli designated to oversee the inquiry.
"We will proceed with the investigation."

De Moraes, fifty, was the Supreme Court's newest member, a former prosecutor who had been appointed several times
to both state and federal offices in left-leaning administrations
by Lula and his future running mate Geraldo Alckmin. He liked
giving the impression of being his own man: as the country's
justice minister, he traveled to Paraguay for a photo op in which
he hacked at marijuana plants with a machete, while the pho-
tographer tried to keep other officials out of the frame so as to
leave the impression his subject was on a solo mission.

Now what was becoming known as the "Fake News Inquiry"
presented a novel opportunity to act as investigator, prosecutor,
and judge in cases of his own making. To conduct his inquest,
de Moraes bypassed the federal ministries with investigative
capacities, enlisting instead a military intelligence service and
the São Paulo police, an early indication that he saw Bolsonaro
and his sons as a potential obstacle if not a target.

The inquiry expanded to cover seemingly anyone who had
spoken caustically about government officials, political opponents, or the court itself. (Even though Brazil's constitution

144   guarantees "freedom of expression," judges have frequently recognized its limits when balanced against other governmental
objectives.) A magazine that mentioned the court's chief justice
in connection to a corruption scandal, quoting from documents
journalists determined were authentic and filed as part of a legal
proceeding, was forced to take down the article and was nonetheless fined $26,000 for not doing so quickly enough. When a
video leaked of a Bolsonaro cabinet meeting in which his education minister was seen saying he wanted to "put these bums
in jail, starting with the Supreme Court," de Moraes issued an
order giving the minister five days to provide "clarification,"
with a threat of criminal penalty. After Bolsonaro made comments suggesting an unproven link between vaccines and AIDS,
de Moraes opened an inquiry into that, too, because the president "used the modus operandi of mass dissemination schemes
in social networks." A right-wing former federal legislator had
his home raided for comments made in social-media posts and
interviews, including a characterization of Lula's supporters as
"LGBT, drug addicts, drug dealers, bank robbers." De Moraes
ordered him placed under house arrest as a form of preventa-
tive detention for "criminal hate speech contrary to democratic institutions and elections." Under a judge's order, both
Facebook and Twitter removed accounts the court said had been
involved in spreading disinformation.

    While critics characterized these actions as the product of
an unconstitutional power grab, with some even likening it to
the abuse of power that occurred under Brazil's military dictatorship, de Moraes defended his work in only the most abstract
terms. "It cannot be allowed, in a democratic country like Brazil,

where institutions have operated freely for thirty years, that, because you do not like a decision, you preach the closure of a republican institution, the death of a minister, the death of relatives," he said.

It took two and a half years for de Moraes to conclude his sprawling investigation. When he did, in August 2021, he identified eleven criminal offenses of which he believed Bolsonaro to be guilty. Several, like slanderous denunciation, were identified as crimes in Brazil's penal code. Others, like inciting the subversion of the political or social order, had been established in the country's dictatorship-era national-security law. Others, related to false claims Bolsonaro had made about Brazilian voting machines, were grounded in the country's electoral laws, and required the cooperation of the Superior Electoral Court.

Bolsonaro never formally faced the charges, which hung over him as he prepared to run for a second term. De Moraes was unrepentant about his investigation. "Justice is blind but it is not stupid, everyone knows what happened in 2018, the mechanism used in the elections," he said in a Supreme Court hearing. "We are not going to allow these digital militias to try again to destabilize the elections." Left unsaid was the fact that the next year de Moraes would assume the electoral court's presidency, as part of the standard rotation that had already cycled him through the court as a substitute judge, then a full member and vice president. The timing meant that de Moraes would begin a two-year term just as the 2022 election season began. It set up the prospect of a tug-of-war over election disinformation waged not by suasion but by competing constitutional powers, between an elected president who might be able to put the muscle of the state, including the military and security apparatus, against a court that had anointed itself the nation's primary arbiter of truth.

Bolsonaro began the day of August 16, 2022, announcing he would again seek the presidency. He flew to the mid-sized industrial city of Juiz de Fora, choosing the same street where he had been stabbed while campaigning four years earlier, to deliver a speech studded with biblical references "giving thanks for the second life." That evening, after leading supporters in a motorcycle convoy through Juiz de Fora, Bolsonaro was back in Brasilia, six hundred miles to the northwest, to grudgingly pay tribute to a man just a year earlier he had publicly called a "scoundrel" and who would now emerge, in many respects, as the biggest opponent of his reelection.

In a subterranean courtroom at the electoral court's head-quarters, one of a series of windowless auditoriums whose white roofs sprouted from the ground like a trio of button mush-rooms, Alexandre de Moraes was formally inaugurated as president of the electoral court.

It took only days for their ambitions to clash. After a Brasilia news site published leaked transcripts of a private WhatsApp group shared by pro-Bolsonaro businessmen in which they bantered about supporting a coup if Lula were to be elected, de Moraes had their offices raided, bank accounts frozen, and phone records seized, without ever filing charges. "What crime? It is clearly an operation to intimidate any notorious figure from taking a political position in favor of Bolsonaro or against the left," responded Bolsonaro's son Eduardo, a federal deputy in

the midst of his own reelection campaign. "This is an attack on
democracy in the middle of an election campaign. Censorship.
No other word!"

But de Moraes had assumed more than just another prosecutor's office. In the tower above his courtroom—ten stories of
dark glass that rose from stubby concrete pylons and captured
the hard sun of the Brazilian highlands to shimmer like an undu-
lating parenthesis—it became clear how much the organization
he was taking over had transformed itself since Bolsonaro was
first elected president.

In August 2019, the Supreme Electoral Court had assigned
twenty-nine staffers to a new Counter Disinformation Program,
emphasizing that its actions were "centered on non-regulatory
and multi-sectoral strategies." But that commitment was complicated just a few months later, when the court appeared to put
legal force behind a resolution declaring "the disclosure or sharing of facts that are known to be untrue or seriously decontextu-
alized that affect the integrity of the electoral process, including
the voting, counting, and totaling of votes, is prohibited."

The court set out to make itself a hub for an emerging
fact-checking culture across Brazilian media. It designated
nine "verification institutions" and collected their work on a
government-hosted "Fact or Rumor" website, negotiating with
mobile providers to ensure users would not be charged for data
when accessing the page. (Rumor: "Election is annulled if more
than 51 percent of votes are invalid." Fact: "Electronic voting machine media was found inside a toilet in Juiz de Fora.")
During the 2020 elections, in which mayors in every Brazilian
city were on the ballot, the page was visited more than 13 million times.

The court had a willing partner in WhatsApp, which was unusually central in Brazilian life, thanks in part to the fact that it allowed users to bypass the costly per-message fees charged by mobile carriers. (One study determined it was fifty-five times more expensive to send a text message in Brazil than the United States.) Company executives claim no ability to monitor content shared by users on the encrypted messaging platform, which effectively frees them from any potential burden to control harmful speech. Rather than moderating content, WhatsApp vowed to Brazilian authorities, it would police behavior. The cardinal rule was an existing policy against "bulk messaging" by users, which WhatsApp attempted to strengthen by placing new limits on the number of recipients and ability to forward. Because accounts were associated with phone numbers rather than individuals or institutions, WhatsApp did not face the same risk of antagonizing prominent figures by removing them from the service that Twitter or Facebook did.

WhatsApp agreed to collaborate with the court to develop a chatbot trained to answer voter questions about key election dates and polling-place locations. More than a million Brazilians used the chatbot over the course of the 2020 elections, helping to identify 752 instances of disinformation. The court also developed an "extrajudicial" channel over which the company could work with Brazilian authorities to investigate and potentially prosecute those who used the platform to violate electoral laws. Over the course of the 2020 municipal elections, WhatsApp banned 1,042 accounts as a result of infractions reported through the court.

In August 2021, the court revealed its plans for the following year's elections, when the presidency, all of Congress, and every state's governor would be on the ballot. The court announced it would make the Counter Disinformation Program permanent, devoting new resources as it developed "medium and long-term strategies for 'immunization' against disinformation." To do so, the court transformed itself partly into a content studio, with a particular focus on "'prophylactic' prebunking actions" that would "reduce citizens' susceptibility to disinformation by exposing examples of how disinformation operates." Court staff began releasing a torrent of content that demonstrated unusual fluency in the patois of the internet: slick infographics, a podcast, and an "Electoral Justice" YouTube channel that offered one series of video explainers narrated entirely in a whisper intended to provoke autonomous sensory meridian response, and another in which the host disassembles an electronic voting machine to show its inner workings.

Throughout 2022, it became nearly impossible to turn on a computer in Brazil and not find oneself, sooner or later, encountering the court. It arranged for TikTok to place warnings on election-related hashtags, reminding users of its policies against "harmful misleading information," and integrated its "Fact or Rumor" research with the WhatsApp chatbot so voters would not have to leave the app for access. Other elements, invisible to users, became part of the new piping of the Brazilian internet: a Disinformation Alert System created a channel to automate the process of notifying platforms like Facebook and Twitter of content the court considered problematic. The messaging app Telegram, run from Dubai by its two Russian founders, participated only after being threatened with having its service blocked entirely within Brazil if it did not accede to the court's demands.

The court traced its authority to regulate content back to a 1965 electoral code declaring "voting can be nullified when distorted by falsehood, fraud, coercion . . . or use of propaganda process." But the code, enacted by a newly installed military dictatorship more attuned to Cold War repression than electoral competition, never defined "propaganda." (The word has a less sinister connotation in Portuguese.) "At that time, what was in and what was not was self-evident," says Francisco Brito Cruz, a legal scholar who is coauthor of the 2019 book *Electoral Law in the Digital Era.* "They never defined. They didn't need to. But this is a big problem in the online sphere." Only in 2006 did lawmakers first amend the electoral code to acknowledge the internet, extending some basic disclosure requirements to digital communication. A 2013 reform, enacted by lawmakers with little controversy, enabled the court to order, "at the request of the offended party, the removal of publications that contain aggressions or attacks on candidates on websites, including social networks." Lawmakers never grappled with the diversity of platforms that could host such content, the variegated processes for removing it, and how the policies might apply in an environment where the power of communication did not just rest with those entities under the court's traditional oversight.

In the years after the 2018 WhatsApp scandal, dozens of proposals circulated through the National Congress to "regulate fake news" but none of them became law. Instead, the court kept granting itself new powers. In 2021, the court stretched the grounds for removal to cover "facts that are known to be untrue or seriously out of context that affect the integrity of the electoral process, including the voting, counting, and totaling of votes." Just days before the second round of voting in 2022, the

court announced it could now proactively demand content be
taken down with a simple order, with ongoing fines of at least
$20,000 to the hosting entity—likely the operator of a website
or a social-media network or platform on which the material
appeared—for every hour of noncompliance.

Every Tuesday evening and Thursday morning during the
election season, when the court's members met in plenary session, they put on a forceful display of their authority. The threat
of a political execution hung over every session: months before
taking office, de Moraes had asserted that spreading online disinformation would be ground for the court to strike a candidate
for any office from the ballot. As he presided from his underground lair, it was just about impossible for anyone to look at de
Moraes, with his shaved head and intense, deep-set eyes, wear-
ing head-to-toe black, including a judge's cape, and not think of
either a comic-book hero or Bond villain, depending on one's
perspective.

The semiweekly sessions became as reliable a source of
campaign-shaping news as the candidates' speeches, rallies,
or televised debates, and the court seemed to bully its way into
every campaign event that took place elsewhere. As Bolsonaro
departed Brazil less than two weeks before the first round of
voting, to attend the funeral of Queen Elizabeth II in London and
the United Nations General Assembly in New York, the court
issued an injunction against using footage from the trip in ads.
Access to such imagery was a function of Bolsonaro's government position, argued judge Benedito Gonçalves, and deploying
it in the campaign context "could hurt the equality of conditions between candidates." Newspapers counted the number of
court "actions" in state-level campaigns as an indicator of how

nationalized each race had become. (On Fridays, the YouTube channel released a new episode of "Then That's It!" in which a casually dressed host summarized the week's judgments from a space with an inexplicable rec-room vibe.)

Having the planet's most aggressive election administrator on their side did little to affect how Bolsonaro's opponents approached the election. Several coalitions covering a broad swath of Brazilian civil society, with backing from parts of the business establishment, were formed with the recognition that ultimately disinformation would move too quickly, and too stochastically, for any government to successfully police it. "I've heard, personally, dozens of times why the electronic voting machine is safe, technically. I've seen videos and stuff," says Caio Tendolini, a São Paulo native who in 2014 worked as the digital-mobilization director for the presidential nominee of Brazil's Socialist Party. "Usually the lie is way more attractive."

Afterward, Tendolini started a project recruiting local activists to run for city council ("from the streets to the ballot box") in his native São Paulo, and then helped found Instituto Update to serve as a hub for political innovation across Latin America. After the 2018 elections, he began to think more about how the same digital networks he had viewed as vehicles for greater grassroots involvement had become vectors for disinformation to spread, often at a cost to the popular politics he espoused. "He is one of the most sophisticated campaigners using WhatsApp and messaging platforms to intervene with the bad actors, actually meeting the problem where it's at," says Jiore Craig. "I hope that the tactics he's using make their way to the US."

Over the course of 2022, Tendolini ran a series of digital campaigns, officially nonpartisan but nevertheless aimed at blocking Bolsonaro from winning a second term. The campaigns focused on various digital subcultures that were united in one attribute. "Most of them don't like politics, they're not consuming hard news on policy pages, but if you are able to build ecosystems that talk about the issues," he says, "you can emulate an echo-chamber effect." For a campaign to register very young voters ahead of a May deadline, Tendolini's organization approached talent agencies representing online influencers, but made clear he was not looking for big celebrities. "We wanted this to be building from the bottom up," he says. "It's about scale but I think it's also about [the] messenger."

Instead he recruited about 120 figures with small but deep footprints, of as few as 10,000 followers—the types of influencers whose names would likely be unknown by anyone who did not follow them. But they usually had geographically compact audiences, which would allow Tendolini's organization to target them more narrowly. They were paid to develop posts aimed at reversing "low political self-esteem," which polls and focus groups had shown was often the primary reason that teenagers did not participate. (In Brazil, voting is allowed from the age of sixteen and becomes compulsory at eighteen.) Then Tendolini's group paid to promote those posts, primarily on Instagram and TikTok, to get in front of like-minded audiences. Even so, the designated register-to-vote hashtag had its own life, promoted by the pop singer Anitta and reality-show celebrity Juliette and then by American actors Leonardo DiCaprio and Mark Ruffalo. Two million sixteen- and seventeen-year-olds registered to vote in 2022, increasing their share of the electorate by nearly 50 percent.

In the fall, Tendolini began planning to deploy a similar tactic to push back against election-fraud conspiracies. If polls

154   continued to show Lula with a significant lead, Tendolini suspected that the Bolsonaro camp's messaging—which tended to
seesaw between baselessly denigrating his opponent (including as a Satanist with ties to organized crime), and those on the
democratic apparatus that appeared poised to put him back in
office—would shift fully toward attacks on the system. "They're
always happening, both of them together," says Tendolini, but as
defeat grew near "the priority for them on those messages will
change very dynamically."

Again Tendolini was thinking about how to build new ecosystems for every contingency. "The most important audience
is the audience that might vote for those who are claiming that
the elections can be fraudulent, but don't trust specifically what
those people say," he says. "They're the people that, if there's a
call-out 'Let's go to the streets' or 'Let's, you know, do something crazy,' these people are persuadable in the sense of 'Just
stay home, you don't want the social chaos or the financial
instability.'"

By the summer of 2022, due in large part to a carefully cultivated digital presence, Guilherme Boulos had become one of
the biggest stars of the Brazilian left. In 2020, he had shocked
pollsters by finishing second in the initial round of the mayoral
race, qualifying for the runoff. Afterward, he bypassed a possible campaign for governor of São Paulo to run instead for the
lower house of Congress, which brought him for the first time
into the federal sphere. "What we need to do this year are anti-
depressant campaigns," said Gallindo, who shot a campaign
video called *Invading Hearts* in which Boulos did little more than
hug strangers on the street. "People are depressed. We need to

work on joy, for people to feel that they are part of the change."
While running as the candidate of a smaller party, Boulos nonetheless threw his support behind Lula. It was expected that
in return Boulos would be able to run for mayor again in 2024
with Workers Party backing. Should he win that office, he would
emerge as Lula's natural heir in the next open contest for the
presidency. As part of the arrangement, Boulos was named general coordinator of Lula's campaign in São Paulo and was able to
place some of his advisers in its headquarters.

Gallindo joined Lula's communications team, putting him
for the first time in the headquarters of a major, well-funded
national campaign. There were resources for production and
distribution of media, and also a new tool for fighting disinformation: attorneys. The Superior Electoral Court's aggressive approach to policing disinformation had introduced a term
to the tactical vocabulary for candidates or parties. Instead of
going on offense against an opponent, mounting a defense, or
trying to change the subject, they could "judicialize" the conflict by filing a proposed action with the court, or seeking other
recourse through the legal system. "Now with the internet,
campaigns have kind of a frontline of producing content, and a
frontline of removing content," says Brito Cruz, who heads the
InternetLab research center in São Paulo. "This is a market, and
it is huge. Campaigns really, really spend on that."

For Lula's campaign that often meant reporting content it
claimed was false or misleading, with a request for it to be taken
down (if it was on the internet) or to be granted equal time out
of an opponent's block of dedicated airtime. On one fairly unexceptional day in August, the court received fifteen different filings from the two Brasilia law firms that together represented

156   the coalition backing Lula's candidacy. They were as long as forty-five pages each, chockablock with screenshots and legalistic debunkings of their contents. "Therefore, the use of a health problem—voice hoarseness—combined with the act of drinking water during speeches to lead voters to the distorted understanding that former President Lula would be drunk, reveals a frivolous and offensive conduct to the image of the candidate, evidencing that the posts, in fact, are a campaign of propagation of fake news with the purpose of violating the fairness of the electoral process," read a typical filing.

Bolsonaro's lawyers pushed back where they could before the court and counterattacked elsewhere in the legal sphere. Bolsonaro appealed to the court to investigate what he said was an imbalance in radio ads, violating the parity guaranteed to candidates under the country's equal-time laws, and when de Moraes declined to do so (labeling the vague claim an "expressly inept request") the president reportedly considered asking for the election to be postponed. There was a hint of early plans to judicialize future elections. When the web domain bolsonaro .com.br—an address once controlled by the politician himself, who appears simply to have allowed its registration to lapse— fell into the hands of a Bolsonaro critic, the federal justice minister ordered a federal police investigation into the new, largely satirical site for a "crime against the honor" of the president for "such a direct and rude attack."

After Bolsonaro significantly overperformed polls in the first round of voting, one of the president's top congressional allies introduced a bill that would criminalize bad polling by making the release of a survey that differed from official results beyond more than the margin of error a federal offense punishable by up to ten years in prison. That proposal, which even if swiftly enacted could not take effect in time to affect the 2022 race, demonstrated the extent to which campaigns viewed judicialization as just a new, seemingly high-minded addition to the public-relations toolbox.

In August, Lula's campaign faced a bombardment of groundless claims portraying him as hostile to Christianity. His advisers recognized that even by denying or correcting them he would be helping to move the debate away from his favored terrain of economic policy and onto Bolsonaro's. Even after Lula publicly insisted that "it is not part of my political culture to establish any principle of holy war in politics," his campaign faced internal pressure from supporters who believed he needed to be more aggressive. "There is a narrative that is being spread within the churches to demonize the figure of former president Lula," Paulo Marcelo Schallenberger, a pastor serving as Lula's liaison to other evangelicals, told a newspaper reporter. "It is necessary for the campaign to make a counterattack and a more direct nod to evangelicals."

So after a week of avoiding the matter, Lula finally responded by having his lawyers challenge Twitter and Facebook posts whose caption declared that Lula supported "invasions of churches and persecution of Christians." Among all the pieces of religious disinformation that circulated, this complaint targeted the one that had been shared by Eduardo Bolsonaro. "It's always case by case, and the criterion is what gets more political gain," says Gallindo. "You know, it's political. It's not about the content."

The gamesmanship around the court's actions pointed to the underlying futility of a system in which responsibility to

158   police misinformation rested with an arm of the state. Some in Washington who struggled to get tech companies to take their problems seriously might have briefly dreamed about an independent government agency with such broad reach and enforcement authority. But having those actions delivered by judicial fiat did not make the job of campaigners any more straightforward. The courts did not remove the disinformation conflict from the political sphere; they just created a new sphere in which traditional political actors had even less control.

Two weeks after Lula filed his challenge, the court ruled in his favor, ordering that the posts be immediately removed and instituting a future fine of approximately $10,000 should Bolsonaro post the content again. Ultimately Lula's attorneys had made the proper legal calculation. But his communications strategists had probably made the wrong political one. By then, nearly everyone who would have seen the original posts likely already had, and Bolsonaro's office of hate was already onto something new. All Lula's campaign had accomplished was twice more returning the subject to the news by creating a fresh story around the court's actions. "I think we hit it and made it bigger," says Gallindo. "Sometimes you just make the problem bigger than it is."

A Permanent Campaign

Right around the time on November 8, 2022, that polls were closing in Georgia, the state that would once again determine the balance of power in the United States Senate after the midterm elections, Jiore Craig set her passionfruit LaCroix on the wood coffee table in her temporary Washington home and curled her suede loafers onto the faux-leather sofa. On her laptop, she opened Rumble, a video-sharing platform that promoted itself as a freewheeling alternative to YouTube, and remained a hub for right-wing networks that struggled to hold a place on cable and satellite services, as her other hand toyed with the television remote control. For the past six weeks, Craig had been living out of an Airbnb apartment, as the generic monochromatic still lifes framed on the walls could attest, and still did not know how to fully command its technology offerings. She frantically texted the unit's owner in search of the Roku password that would let her control the television. "I want to watch Newsmax more than I want to watch Fox, while on Rumble I'm watching the Right Side Broadcasting Network, which is just like a totally alternate universe," said Craig. "I don't even watch mainstream coverage during a day like today."

Election nights are typically a time for camaraderie on campaigns, a moment where there is little left to do but share in the emotional release. But over the course of the five years Craig had been working in domestic politics, those nights had grown gradually more dreadful. First there was a pandemic, which scattered her Greenberg Quinlan Rosner team across the country. Then the election itself came to represent for counter-disinformation researchers not the end of a cycle but the likely beginning of a new, more dangerous phase. "It got harder to say to our teams on election nights, 'Come in, we'll order pizza, have fun,' right?" she said, as she awaited delivery of a grain bowl. "You know, it's not fun."

Craig and her colleagues never really slowed down following the 2020 election. Over two months, they watched diffuse allegations about supposed voting irregularities transmute into a conspiracy theory about "rigged elections," then a violent invasion of the seat of power and a multiyear revisionist drive to redefine what had happened at the Capitol on January 6. The federated structure she had helped to erect for the Strategic Victory Fund in 2019 was tied to party committees whose staffing and funding were built to move the voters necessary to win elections, not hold up one side of an open-ended debate over the elections' basic legitimacy. What began as a job advising campaigns to track and beat back digital misinformation had become the project of uncoiling a nation's endemic paranoia. "I was so burnt out. One person I know had a seizure, another person I know passed out in the shower," said Craig. "There just

wasn't any support. People still don't understand what it is like
to look at these phones all day."

In the spring of 2021, she departed Greenberg Quinlan
Rosner to join the Institute for Strategic Dialogue, a London-
based think tank dedicated to countering extremist networks, where as head of digital integrity she would oversee its
election-related work worldwide. One immediately appealing benefit of joining the fifteen-year-old organization was the
mandatory trauma counseling provided to staff. While living in
London, Craig also began to advise the Archewell Foundation,
even as its founders Prince Harry and Meghan Markle reset-
tled in North America, on their goal of "restoring trust in information." In both instances, Craig welcomed the opportunity to
contribute constructively to worldwide policy debates rather
than just advising American candidates on defense tactics. (She
continued, in a personal capacity, to advise one American electoral campaign.)

"Those sourcing disinformation are experts in maximiz-
ing social media product features and loopholes to achieve
their ends. This is why it is so important to focus on the systemic aspects of social media companies, such as their business
models or product features, geopolitical and commercial interests," Craig told a congressional hearing in the summer of 2022.
"A focus on such systemic dynamics is essential to hold social
media companies and disinformation bad actors accountable.
We cannot just debate which meme is more rooted in fact. We
need to debate which systems at play in disinformation should
change to end the downward spiral of trust that Americans have
started to have in their own democracy, and even more important, in each other."

To that point, Craig had generally kept a low public profile, becoming well-known to nearly everyone who mattered in Democratic politics and largely invisible beyond that. She was scornful of how the mainstream media covered disinformation, with a particular disdain for a burgeoning cohort of reporters who had turned the topic into a beat. Journalists always appeared eager to anoint a new disinformation danger—already it was becoming likely that 2024 would be awash with stories about the danger of artificial-intelligence chatbots and image generators—and, in their zeal to expose dangerous narratives, ended up amplifying them, she thought. Craig also knew how readily those identified in press coverage as "disinformation experts" had become a target of right-wingers who considered the job description mere cover for aspiring censors. After buying Twitter, Elon Musk approvingly responded to a user who said he would "not trust anyone who uses the words 'disinformation' or 'misinformation.'" Musk added, "especially if they say they're an expert at both."

Ahead of the 2022 midterm elections, Craig made a decision to court attention from a press that was portraying the country's first national vote since January 6 as a test for its defenses against disinformation. She tried to use the opportunity to argue for fleeting calm and enduring concern. She appeared live on CNN and Bloomberg, and was quoted by the BBC and Axios, always shifting responsibility back onto the social-media companies she said were failing to police the content distributed on their platforms. "Our teams are strung out picking up the slack of the well-resourced entities that could be doing this kind of work," she told the *New York Times* in an article about YouTube's struggles to control misinformation related to elections in both the United States and Brazil. On the morning before the election, a large portrait of Craig, looking sternly into the camera, appeared in the newspaper's business section.

The next night, she was agonizing over it. "If I had to pick what to be in the *Times* about, I wouldn't have it be about elections. Election disinformation isn't the biggest online harm issue and election disinformation is also not going to be the path to accountability" for tech companies, she said. "It's not just polarizing, it's also not motivating the half of the country who doesn't vote. You know, the people who are busy with the rest of their lives. What's going to motivate change, meaningful change, is going to be things like keeping kids safe online, kids and their mental health, loneliness—that's gonna lead to actual change.

"I think of myself as someone—you know, like, I'm from the Midwest—who is a good messenger, not a political messenger. But the more that you just put yourself on this side of things the more you lose credibility. We're already so short on messengers, right?" Craig went on. "When I say 'we,' I mean those of us who care about a decent and responsible information and a healthy information ecosystem," she said as her eyes drifted back across the three screens in front of her. "Like, I don't even know who the 'we' is at this point anymore."

On each day of Joe Biden's presidency, two sets of reports arrived to shape the White House's view of emerging threats. There was the President's Daily Brief, the classified compendium compiled by the intelligence community and personally handed to the commander-in-chief since the early Cold War, presenting the country's leaders a tour of the global security landscape. The other, drafted by a group of twenty-somethings in Greenberg Quinlan Rosner's digital department and delivered into the email inboxes of many of Biden's top advisers, offered a lens on the domestic political environment. They tracked online chatter about Biden, his son Hunter, Vice President Kamala Harris, and issues of transient interest—Afghanistan during the withdrawal of American personnel from the war zone, student loans as the administration finalized a plan to erase existing debts. They were a valuable legacy of the disinformation defense federation as it became a durable utility for the party and movement, serving its needs both for electioneering and governance. Officials in the highest reaches of Biden's White House came to rely on the reports, including chief of staff Ron Klain, who around a big news event would often send the Democratic National Committee headquarters a query unimaginable barely a half-decade earlier: *What was the committee seeing on the disinformation front?*

For much of the summer of 2022, the subject of that attention was the Inflation Reduction Act. The package, a costly amalgam of new outlays and tax-code changes—aimed largely at fighting climate change, reducing prescription-drug costs, and shrinking the deficit—represented a crowning achievement of Biden's first congressional session leading his party. The monitoring reports Greenberg Quinlan Rosner produced for the federation regularly contained good news for Klain, as what analysts called the "share of voice" around the Inflation Reduction Act was dominated by mainstream and left-leaning sources covering the suspenseful wrangling over Democrats' efforts to consolidate their slight Senate majority behind the bill. Republicans offered only modest appraisals of the bill's

shortcomings. Some were rote criticisms of progressive gover-
nance (spending too much money) and familiar differences of
policy focus (climate investments would distort the country's
energy sector) and others on its opportunistic rebranding (little in the bill could be expected to lower near-term consumer
prices, which polls showed were voters' leading concern).

That changed on August 7. As the Senate prepared to vote
that day on the Inflation Reduction Act, Republicans zeroed
in on a heretofore little-noticed funding mechanism in the
bill. Instead of adjusting tax rates, Democrats had pledged to
raise revenue with more aggressive enforcement of existing
taxes, supported with an additional $80 billion to the Internal
Revenue Service. The majority of that money was expected to
be spent on what the agency calls "program integrity," activity designed to raise more than it costs by getting taxpayers to
pay what they already owe. The IRS would have great leeway in
terms of how that money would be spent, but if applied to fill a
staff emptying out due to retirement it could help to fund up to
86,852 personnel over a decade, a report from Biden's Treasury
Department had calculated. Elsewhere, routine IRS job listings
required agents to "be legally allowed to carry a firearm" and
"willing to use deadly force, if necessary," a prerequisite necessary only for a small number of agents who work on cases
involving matters like drug trafficking. A digital video posted
by Texas Republican Ted Cruz two days before the Senate
vote strung those disparate facts into a lively fiction: "Biden is
building a shadow army of 87,000 new IRS agents to hunt you
down and take your money."

The next day, an unrelated event a thousand miles away
gave momentum to Cruz's allegation. In Palm Beach, Florida,

166   the Federal Bureau of Investigation entered Donald Trump's Mar-a-Lago beach club to execute a search warrant for illegally obtained government records. "After todays [sic] raid on Mar A Lago what do you think the left plans to use those 87,000 new IRS agents for?" Florida Senator Marco Rubio wrote on Twitter. "Not a single one of us is safe," Kari Lake, the Republican nominee for governor in Arizona, added. Over the course of that week, Republican outrage about the Trump investigation fed an increasingly baseless paranoia about the tax compliance, following a familiar trajectory for right-wing attacks. The supposed IRS army became a staple of programming on the Fox News Channel, where later that week Iowa Senator Chuck Grassley was asked about it on the *Fox & Friends* morning show. "Are they going to have a strike force that goes in with AK-15s already loaded, ready to shoot some small businessperson in Iowa?" Grassley speculated.

Democrats across Washington watched with alarm. This new narrative could not derail the bill, which was headed to Biden's desk with the votes of every House Democrat behind the Senate version with the new IRS funding. Three months before the election, however, the Democratic Congressional Campaign Committee's disinformation task force was worried about the electoral impact. After being promoted in the spring of 2021 to serve as the committee's senior adviser for disinformation strategy, Ben Block had set a goal of making the committee self-sufficient in its ability to generate independent analysis to provide candidates and campaigns. When he set out to secure the committee's own stream of monitoring data, some who had helped to assemble the left's disinformation-monitoring federation saw it as an attempt to undermine the unified structure.

Block ended up hiring VineSight, an Israeli firm that used
artificial-intelligence techniques to automate much of the work
that Craig had trained her team at Greenberg Quinlan Rosner
to perform manually. VineSight pulled data from Facebook,
Twitter, Reddit, and YouTube and designed a dashboard that
grouped content by candidate, issue, and generalized sentiment
about the party's reputation, separating Spanish-language
material from that localized to other communities of color.
(Democratic counter-disinformation operatives struggled to
deal with foreign-language material in any systematic way, due
to both the difficulty of translation and the disproportionate use
of closed messaging platforms like WhatsApp for communication in immigrant communities. Upon starting work in a new
district, field organizers on congressional races were encouraged to win entry into invitation-only messaging groups and
submit reports on notable content or trends via a Google form
to Block's team.) Where most social-listening tools could read
only text, VineSight had the capacity to scan images and include
their content in its analysis. So when Musk traded anti-IRA gifs
with another Twitter user—one of them featuring an image of
House Speaker Pelosi holding a Mega Millions lottery check
made out to herself in the value of the spending package—they
contributed to the committee's analysis. "There was no way
of really having eyes on it before, unless you came across it on
your own feed, which, given how my algorithm works, I probably would not," says Block.

Most usefully, VineSight's algorithms were trained to recognize the patterns of virality that preceded a piece of disinformation making the jump from insular corners of the right-wing
internet to places where it could influence persuadable voters or

168   demoralize parts of the Democratic coalition. "We wanted to see if we could potentially break the cycle," says Devorah Adler, who served as research director for Barack Obama's first presidential campaign and later effectively became VineSight's representative in Washington. "In order to stop something from going viral, you have to find it very, very early."

Researchers at Greenberg Quinlan Rosner started hearing about the IRS agents whenever they asked about the Inflation Reduction Act in focus groups, and eventually assessed it the most detrimental criticism of the bill. There was also visible real-world impact. A little more than a week after Grassley's interview, the IRS confirmed that "an abundance of misinformation and false social media postings, some of them with threats directed at the IRS and its employees," had forced the agency to embark on a "comprehensive" security review. Treasury Secretary Janet Yellen issued an unusual public letter to the IRS commissioner directing that the new funds be directed to programs aimed at wealthy individuals and corporate taxpayers. "This means that, contrary to the misinformation from opponents of this legislation, small business or households earning $400,000 per year or less will not see an increase in the chances that they are audited," Yellen wrote. The IRS itself tried to correct false impressions about how it operated, having its criminal-investigative division speak to reporters about the conditions under which agents carried firearms.

But by that point there was no way to stop the IRS narrative, which seemed to follow a pattern Craig had first identified when the murder of George Floyd by a Minneapolis police officer in 2020 drew newfound national attention on matters of race relations and police brutality. Immediately after Floyd's death,

the most-shared articles on Facebook about the incident and
the subsequent protests and riots came from mainstream and
left-leaning voices, as readers sought out credible information
from sources like NBC News and the *Washington Post*. Once the
initial rush of news interest subsided, however, right-leaning
voices like Daily Wire and Breitbart had wrested back what analysts called "share of voice" on topics related to the Floyd killing. Many were conspiracy theories that absolved the police,
such as the baseless claim Floyd had died of a drug overdose or
that his death had been faked as part of a supposed plot coordinated by left-wing donor George Soros to rally "Antifa" activists
behind a criminal-justice reform agenda. Just as those fictions
were more compelling than a debate over policing reforms, the
"shadow army of IRS agents" narrative displaced coverage of the
Inflation Reduction Act's provisions, flipping the online share
of voice toward right-leaning publishers.

The White House had recognized the lies jeopardized the
success of the policy itself. Attacks on the Affordable Care Act,
both grounded in policy differences and myths like "death pan-
els," inspired Republican-led state governments to hold back
their full participation while their congressional allies worked
to repeal the law. (These persisted for nearly a decade after its
2010 passage until eventually most Republicans acknowledged
they could not agree on a plan to unwind a law that had become
accepted as part of the safety-net fabric.) Heightened distrust
of the IRS would likely complicate the objective of increased
taxpayer compliance, and undermine the public support necessary to sustain continued legislative support for the project.
Debunking the lie about the 87,000 agents would be crucial to
Biden's governing agenda.

But the Democratic Congressional Campaign Committee made a determination that the disinformation was not worth confronting directly. "Without engaging directly with right-wing framing, emphasize that this bill will be financed by cracking down on rich tax cheats and making the wealthiest corporations in America pay their fair share—and that no Americans making less than $400,000 a year will see new taxes or additional IRS audits as a result of this bill," Greenberg Quinlan Rosner digital-communication director Jake Engle wrote in an August 18 memo to the DCCC. "Discredit right-wing claims about the IRS as a desperate attempt to distract from the economic benefits of the bill, which the GOP opposed. Point specifically to GOP efforts to strip the bill of its insulin price caps, which Democrats supported."

When the committee launched its disinformation task force in 2019, it had been very guarded with the reports it received from Greenberg Quinlan Rosner. There was the perennial fear of internal deliberations leaking to the press in a way that unmasked its process or revealed vulnerabilities. The greatest fear, however, was overreaction. Politicians tended to assume that when they heard from their campaign arm on a given topic, it was to communicate the committee's priorities, and they needed to do something about it. Throughout 2020, unless there was a need for urgent action by a candidate or campaign, Block shared information by discreetly incorporating it—"baking in," as he liked to say—into talking points or other messaging guidance being routinely distributed by the campaign. But members of Congress clamored for more detail, and the committee made a decision as it began its 2022 work to

hand over reports and other tracking data to members and their
staffs. "We're being very open with our candidates and trust-
ing them not to share," Block explained then. Democratic officials and candidates largely stuck to the guidance they received.
(There were a few notable exceptions. "Have you heard wild
claims about '87,000 IRS agents'?" began one of two Twitter
posts on the topic from Pennsylvania's Dwight Evans, a member
of the tax-writing Ways and Means Committee.) "Sometimes
there is an inclination to chase attacks unnecessarily," reflects
Engel, "but I think our side has generally been good at staying
focused on this issue."

Days after Biden won the presidency, Bully Pulpit Interactive
began marketing the process it had used to help elect him. "To
better arm our clients against the spread of misinformation,
we're drawing on our work with the Biden campaign to launch
Parry, a framework for tracking, understanding, and responding to disinformation campaigns using sophisticated analytics,
survey research, and digital ads," Jessica Reis and Joe Ste. Marie
wrote in a Medium post promoting the new service.

They found interest from corporate clients subject to
attacks that could turn off potential consumers or investors,
and nonprofit organizations trying to tackle large, intracta-
ble problems where public opinion showed scientific expertise
growing less trusted. For the advocacy groups Environmental
Defense Action Fund and Climate Power, Bully Pulpit tested fifteen narratives that were raising doubts among people who recognized climate change was a problem but were unconvinced
of the need for urgent action. Many of those that landed in the

upper-right quadrant of the harm index related to the idea that climate-related policies were explicitly designed to raise gas prices.

A similar process helped the Ad Council design public-service announcements aimed at the approximately 100 million Americans who expressed uncertainty about receiving a COVID-19 vaccine. Bully Pulpit's research demonstrated that an ad campaign might not succeed in assuaging doubts about the cost of getting the vaccine among those skeptical of the government that regulated its development, but it could help persuade them to see the benefits of doing so by showing emotionally resonant images about a return to normal life (a couple hugging their grandchildren, a college football stadium full on game day).

From a marketing perspective, the timing could not have been better to convince Democrats to undertake a similar push for their candidates and causes. Over the previous four years, the party had become so alert to the presence of disinformation that they were inclined to see it everywhere. Disinformation was at the root of Trump's political identity. It was the cause of his first victory and of the closeness of his second, the reason he twice escaped accountability through impeachment, the basis for Democratic underperformance in 2020 at the hands of an electorate convinced they wanted to "defund the police," and the motivation for a right-wing insurrection on January 6. The future risked worse. In the words of Democratic operative and Media Matters founder David Brock, "Misinformation is an existential threat to democracy."

Yet despite offering perhaps the most persuasive case study of how a campaign could proactively counter it, Bully Pulpit

could not find a single political client willing to pay for Parry.
All the research proved pricey: a large benchmark-style poll,
updated weekly, and a run of focus groups to help make sense of
it all. But above all, the entire project was dependent on generating a large new digital-advertising budget—in addition to whatever a campaign was planning to spend for its standard positive
and negative messaging. Perhaps no candidate, other than one
running for president or for statewide office under exception-
ally friendly circumstances, could justify deploying it, or would
have the time and money.

The party's best tacticians approached campaigns through
the lens of the modern databases known as the voter file, an
amalgamation of registration records augmented with consumer data—a portrait of the electorate both as a whole and
distilled to the individual. The voter file was a useful framework for observing, and trying to measure, the effect of one's
own communication, since the campaign knew how it had been
targeted. It was ill-suited for recognizing the flow of material that originated from an unknown or uncertain source and
traveled through opaque networks the campaign did not control. "Propaganda is kind of like in a gaseous state," observes
Will Robinson, the media consultant who first brought Craig
into domestic campaigns. "You can't grab it, and so people act
like it's not really happening." The circle around Trump, whose
2016 campaign never did any significant traditional voter contact, adjusted easily to the new environment; his opponents did
not. "In the age of the voter file, everyone wanted everything
automated," Craig says. "I can't tell you how many dollars have
probably been wasted by people trying to match the voter file to
Twitter data."

That was not the only area where scientific rigor and empiricist logic had proven ill-suited for the murky sphere where digital disinformation moves. Field experiments had helped to answer many foundational questions for which even a generation ago a multibillion-dollar business relied on little more than folk wisdom: Is a get-out-the-vote postcard more effective than a robocall? Do professional call centers work better than volunteer phone banks? Does it matter if canvassers are from the same community as the voters whose doors they knock?

Those who controlled the left's funding sources recognized the value of such randomized-control trials, known as "RCTs," and began to reflexively demand it as a prerequisite for any support. "The donor community put a flaming hoop in front of us, like 'you have to jump through this.' And that flaming hoop is RCTs," says David Goldstein of We Defend Truth, which used such experiments to assess the effectiveness of its gifs and memes aimed at Trump supporters. Experiments were effective for measuring the types of voter behavior researchers had tracked before, like registration and turnout, or short-term persuasion, but not necessarily new ones, like pulling back a fellow citizen from the rim of a conspiracy-theory rabbit hole. Anything expected to move virally was by its nature difficult to control under experimental conditions. "An RCT is supposed to help inform the work, and unfortunately we've moved to a place where it dictates the work," says Goldstein. "It's tremendously damaging, because you never ever get real innovation out of an RCT. You just can't, because innovation comes from moving everything in a certain direction or rethinking everything from the ground up."

The innovations so central to progressive successes in the
Obama years were not only inadequate to the new challenges,
but had become constraints. "We Democrats are stuck in the
innovator's dilemma," Robinson says. "We're doing incremen-
tal change. Literally, 'let's see what happens if we put the stamp
on the inside of the envelope?' We need to do a new model. And
we're not doing a new model."

The disinformation panic masked a deeper agitation among
political professionals, who as a class had never fully adjusted to
the changes the internet was making on the practice of democracy. Their vocation was closely tied to a historical moment—
when the power to reach large audiences was consolidated
among elite actors who largely adhered to rules and norms
setting some standard for political speech—that by 2016 had
clearly passed. "Disinformation" became an outlet for all the
free-floating anxieties related to passage into a new, unfamil-
iar environment. Unlike policymakers, political operatives were
not really concerned with truth or falsity; they were perfectly
at ease when the primary vectors of disinformation were senators or cable-news networks, whose sensibilities and pressure
points they understood. But when their opponents were anonymous, placeless social-media accounts operating from ambigu-
ous motivations they had little to offer. When they spoke about
the vexing challenge of disinformation, they were acknowledging a newfound powerlessness. They had lost control of the
means of communication.

On a mild early November evening, Ben Block sat at a sidewalk
table at a bar near his Washington home. His work on behalf

of Democratic congressional candidates in the 2022 midterm elections was effectively done, and he was looking forward to a college-basketball game that night; for the first time in a while he would be able to watch a sporting event without much fear that at some point his attention would be forcibly redirected to something moving on his laptop's disinformation-tracking dashboard. It would take weeks to finish counting votes in all the nation's congressional races, and even though Republicans would end up retaking control of the House after four years in the minority, the election cycle was shaping up as an unexpected success for Democrats. They would hold the Senate and a series of battleground-state governorships. Media coverage pointed out that Republican candidates who promoted the election-denialist "Big Lie" were shut out of battleground-state offices, including governor, attorney general, and secretary of state, where they would have had a role in overseeing future vote counts.

Over the coming months, the leadership of the Democratic Congressional Campaign Committee would change. Block had already, unusually, weathered two different changes in regime at the committee and would have to decide if he wanted to stick around for a third. He had always been cheerfully pollyannaish about his work, perhaps the result of coming to it from the digital-fundraising realm and its perpetual cycle of optimization, rather than the bleakly zero-sum realities of geopolitics. But over a beer, Block had trouble summoning any sort of optimism.

Elon Musk's purchase of Twitter had just been officially completed, and Block observed the impact almost immediately. He had previously considered Twitter a more upright

collaborator than Meta's Facebook in efforts to safeguard its
platform, even as it was comparatively shorthanded in that
work. Block chuckled as he recalled that when Twitter officials
sought to justify their inaction over one enforcement request
or another, they often observed they employed fewer people
worldwide than Meta did in Ireland alone. (This appeared to be
no longer true although it may have been years earlier.) Now,
Block observed, there was no longer anyone left even to half-
heartedly mount that wan defense.

Shortly, Musk would tap friendly journalists to act as a
conduit to publish what he grandly called the Twitter Files, a
curated selection of internal documents from the company's
archive demonstrating that "Big Tech is out to get conservatives,
and is increasingly willing to undermine First Amendment values by complying with the Biden Administration's directives
that suppress freedom of speech online," as summarized by
Ohio Representative Jim Jordan. This rhetorical legerdemain,
conflating government authorities, political actors, and private companies, obscured the fact that most of the documents
showed something very different. Here were high-profile cus-
tomers whom a company had aggressively courted to use its
service making an earnest effort to understand the company's own rules while beseeching it to enforce them, albeit only
when it served their interests. At the Democratic committees,
the release of private correspondence—including exchanges
with Angus King's 2018 Senate campaign and the Democratic
National Committee's Tim Durigan—was viewed as an act of
war, a signal that any good-faith cooperation with the company would be heretofore impossible. Block was ready to give
up on the idea that there was anything campaigners like himself

could do if tech companies insisted on being an active obstacle to their efforts rather than just an unreliable partner. "It's a whole of democracy issue," he said despairingly.

It was a fatalism shared by many of those who had helped to build the left's apparatus for tracking disinformation and mitigating its electoral impact. "I try to fight the dystopian part of this, but it is pretty dystopian, because the speed in which the harms are unfolding, is it matched with our time needed to steer this major ship in the right direction?" says Kristina Wilfore, who moved back to the United States to work on counter-disinformation issues after a decade of practicing politics abroad. "It's a stopgap emergency and whack-a-mole kind of approach. We will win some and will lose some, and will probably start to lose more."

They came to recognize the limited application and marginal value of their tactical interventions, especially as they realized they were combating not just individual mistruths but all-encompassing delusions about how the world worked and the disintegration of any common structure of factual authority. "While the jiujitsu of each individual message, attack, and response is required, the real goal is to short-circuit disinformation at the systemic level," says Tim Chambers of the Dewey Square Group. "Disinformation's core business model and risk-to-reward ratio must be short-circuited over time."

Those short-term and long-term objectives found themselves occasionally in conflict. This was especially true when it came to the question of whether any progress was conceivable without first weakening the businesses that sustain the right-wing disinformation economy—or whether their networks were necessary vectors for correcting the lies they spread.

Media Matters launched a Drop Fox campaign aimed at the network's advertisers, and an Unfox My Cable Box campaign at
the cable providers who carried it. The Check My Ads Institute
advised corporations to navigate to ensure their brands did not
appear on websites that had promoted election disinformation ahead of January 6. "This is a bonfire now," says cofounder
Claire Atkin. "So we have to take away its fuel as well as douse
it." At the same time, however, the Biden campaign was buying ads specifically to run alongside disinformation content on
sites like Breitbart, and We Defend Truth even restored sites
that groups like Check My Ads had convinced advertising platforms to add to a blacklist for their role in January 6–related
disinformation. "The whole thing is about finding people where
they're at," says Goldstein. "I don't know any other way to face
the real world, other than to accept the fact that people we need
to reach go to some really horrible websites. I think we can battle back against that once or if we ever do get our own publishing
ecosystem up and running."

It was there that the counter-disinformation left found some
sort of consensus. Where in past decades Democrats spoke about
the need for their own version of Fox News or Rush Limbaugh,
now they talk about building the type of media outlets that gave
right-leaning publishers such dominance on Facebook. Some of
the most promising projects involved using non-political content to build digital audiences that can be later activated around
political issues. The Accelerate Change Network has used targeted advertising to draw millions of followers to accounts built
around salient identities—immigrants, parents, and domestic
workers—who are served a stream of wholesome content, typically with either an uplift or self-help sensibility. These brands

exist almost exclusively on social media: PushBlack puts videos about black history on TikTok, while Pulso produces Instagram posts about Latino culture. ("Did you know the Aztecs had a great sense of humor?" read one. "Swipe to read about our ancestors.") The independent WorkMoney was founded by longtime labor organizer CJ Grimes in the early days of the coronavirus pandemic as "a not-for-profit group that helps Americans figure out how to navigate the worst economic catastrophe of our lifetimes," by its own self-description. WorkMoney began on Facebook, spending aggressively on advertising to promote its snappy personal-finance advice and valorization of blue-collar work, then used surveys soliciting followers' phone numbers so it could communicate with them directly via text message. These outlets were all officially nonpartisan and obscure about their political orientations—the "About Us" page of the WorkMoney website identified the founder by only her first and middle names and made no mention of her union background—but progressive donors recognized their value. (WorkMoney raised more than $20 million by the end of its second year.) "If you have a friend who's in an abusive relationship, you want to get them out of that relationship. But step one always is make sure that they have the ability to speak with you, the ability to hear information that has not been filtered or vetted by their abuser. And so we have an open line of communication," says Dmitri Mehlhorn.

The only goals that made sense anymore were those set on a distant horizon. "It's our job to win the battle of ideas to protect democracy and inclusive society, and I think in that sense we need to be looking at making sure that media is in the hands of people that believe in truth," says Tom Perriello, a former Virginia congressman who headed the American operations

of the Open Society Foundation, the nonprofit arm of George
Soros's empire. "We probably spent more on it than anyone else.
And I think we'd be the first to say we're not scratching the sur-
face of what needs to be done."

From São Paulo, Caio Tendolini studied the run-up to January
6 and its aftermath, the way online lies had mobilized offline
mobs to reject an election result they did not like. Tendolini
believed he had learned its salient lessons: to begin early by
denying disinformation campaigns aimed at undermining the
country's electoral machinery results any opportunity to gain
a foothold online. He designed a campaign for TikTok and
Instagram called Confia No Brasil ("believe in Brazil") to pre-
emptively define any such effort as patriotic, looking especially
for local sports-minded influencers to promote his message.
Much of it played into Brazil's love of soccer, emphasizing not
its qualities as the beautiful game but its reality as a rule-based
order—the winners win, the losers lose, and everyone accepts a
decision of the referee no matter how much they might wish it
had gone another way.

Early in the election season, Tendolini had marked on his
calendar a number of key dates for the Confia No Brasil program: Independence Day in early September, when President
Jair Bolsonaro would lead massive rallies, parades, and military
displays; the day of the general election and a potential runoff,
either of which could be decisive for the presidency; the World
Cup beginning in November, when patriotically minded crowds
would gather to watch the national team's matches garbed in
its famous canary yellow jerseys; through to the constitution-
ally mandated transfer of power in Brasilia on January 1. "I think

the US example helped us understand the importance of going all the way through a moment where the person who holds office right now and is talking about these things, he's just not there anymore, because then it's different," Tendolini said in September.

Every one of those landmark dates passed without the type of conflagration many had expected to see. (Conveniently for purposes of civic order, Brazil crashed out of the World Cup in the quarterfinals.) Bolsonaro's leftist challenger, Lula da Silva, captured a decisive if not overwhelming victory in both rounds of voting, leading many voices in the country's bien-pensant commentariat to conclude that the entire "fake news" obsession sustained by the country's courts was overblown all along. "Perhaps there was a very self-complacent explanation for Bolsonaro's triumph in 2018: that fake news and massive disinformation campaigns had duped an unsuspecting voter. The result now suggests no. People really choose, they are not deceived," argued João Paulo Charleaux, a longtime journalist and commentator. "Take that ingredient off the table," wrote Cristina Tardáguila, who founded one of Brazil's leading fact-checking websites.

Judge Alexandre de Moraes named Lula the winner on television as his electoral court worked to stamp out online disinformation asserting otherwise. Leading figures in Bolsonaro's party immediately accepted the legitimacy of the result, and although the president never conceded the election he would comply with the result, permitting a transition between governments to proceed. By the last day on Tendolini's calendar, January 1, Bolsonaro had already left the scene, resigning his office ahead of schedule as he departed for Florida in an apparent effort to evade criminal investigators. In his place, a thirty-three-year-old trash-picker and recycling activist represented "the Brazilian people" in placing the symbolic sash on President Lula da Silva. Government officials, diplomats, and journalists all celebrated the peaceful transition of power.

That relief was premature. One week later, as many as 5,000 Brazilians—lured to their capital through WhatsApp and Telegram groups, on TikTok videos and in Twitter posts— descended on the same location, overwhelming security forces and rampaging through the buildings that housed Brazil's Congress, Supreme Court, and presidential offices. As had been the case in Washington almost exactly two years earlier, the January 8 riot and subsequent siege lasted for hours, covered live on television as it unfolded.

Craig watched from London. The following day, she sent a message to Tendolini, with whom she now shared a once-unimaginable experience that was starting to appear as though it might become routine. "The repeat of January 6 that everyone was worried about in the US didn't happen in the US, but it happened pretty much verbatim in Brazil," she says. "I know exactly what his team just went through."

Craig explained how she had managed a similar situation two years earlier, and passed along some messaging guidance about how to publicly frame what had just happened. They commiserated over feeling let down by powerful institutions— some of the world's most highly valued companies, an election regulator with every power that even the most zealous counter-disinformation advocate could imagine. From opposite corners of the Atlantic, they both felt alone on the shore, trying to assess the heaving ocean before them and wondering if there was any reason to still be there when the next big wave hit.

"What it shows more than anything is the fragility of all this," says Craig. "When I think about all the people I know in this space who are really good at this, we've ended up in such different places since we've taken on the fight. I don't know that any of us have moved toward some grand way to work together and solve the problem. I think we've either figured out in what little spot can we make an impact, or we just moved on entirely and tried to live a good life."

Ever since I published my first book with Columbia Global Reports in 2016, its chief, Nick Lemann, has expressed an interest in publishing a follow-up to my book *The Victory Lab*. It took five years for us to figure out what exactly that story was, and I am so pleased that doing so gave me the chance to reunite with a publishing team that feels like coming home to family. Nick Lemann, Jimmy So, Camille McDuffie, Allison Finkel, Courtney Knights, along with Angela Baggetta, have been a pleasure to work with at every turn. I must thank my agent, Larry Weissman, and his partner, Sascha Alper, who first connected me with Columbia Global Reports almost a decade ago and have enabled me to pursue my chosen career for nearly two.

I owe a debt to April White and Jonathan Martin for reading the manuscript, and my kitchen cabinet for ongoing guidance and counsel: James Burnett, Michael Schaffer, and Maggie Haberman. At UCLA, I am grateful to Department of Political Science's Jeff Lewis, Chris Tausanovitch, and, above all, Lynn Vavreck, along with librarians at the Young Research Library. Mary Krause has kept her perpetual cheer as she works to ensure my writing gets in front of the right audience, and Mellissa Meisels kindly agreed to take on one last fact-checking assignment. If not for the reassuring presence of Mercy Maldonado I am not sure I would ever actually get any work done in the first place.

Much thanks to my dear friend Patricia Campos Mello for hand-holding my first foray into Brazilian political reporting, an assignment that allowed me to benefit from both the company and the insight of my São Paulo family: Luisa Belchior,

186   Mauricio Savarese, and Carolina. (May every journalist who arrives in a foreign land on the eve of an election have cousins who cover the country's politics for a living.) My Washington family was always there with a warm welcome on my reporting trips to more familiar environs: Keltie Hawkins, Mike, Eva, and my goddaughter, Eleanor Schaffer.

Nothing would be possible if not for my parents, Bella Brodzki and Henry Issenberg; my sister, Sarina Issenberg; my aunt Gayle Brodzki; in-laws, Susan Bass Levin and Ben Levin; and the Beaubaires: Lisa, David, Maddie, Will, and Charlie. Amy Levin is the finest partner one could have in life, and she was especially understanding as I added a book deadline to a year already full of other disruptions to our life. (Disclosure: Amy did polling work for the Democratic Congressional Campaign Committee during the 2020 and 2022 cycles, but she was not involved in any of the counter-disinformation activities covered in this book.)

The best of those disruptions is our daughter, and this book is dedicated to her. Maxie Luda, I promise I will write a more optimistic one for you soon.

Meme Wars: The Untold Story of the Online Battles Upending Democracy in America (PublicAffairs, 2022) is an engaging account of ten episodes, starting with the Occupy Wall Street protests of 2011, in which outsider communities rallied and organized online to great effect. All of the episodes documented by Joan Donovan, Emily Dreyfuss, and Brian Friedberg begin online but don't end there, and their book in its entirety makes a persuasive case that the decade's most influential political movements had their origins as digital mobs.

How did a single website become arguably the most central institution in global politics? In *Anti-Social Media: How Facebook Disconnects Us and Undermines Our Democracy* (Oxford University Press, 2018), Siva Vaidhyanathan offers a thoughtful assessment of how a single website grew to play so many roles—The Protest Machine, The Surveillance Machine, The Pleasure Machine, and, yes, The Disinformation Machine—and the threat it now poses to the world.

Perhaps the most ambitious effort to map the new decentralized information environment comes from a unique database built by Harvard's Berkman Klein Center. In their *Network Propaganda: Manipulation, Disinformation, and Radicalization in American Politics* (Oxford University Press, 2018), colleagues Yochai Benkler, Robert Faris, and Hal Roberts mine the database to show how much the American right won the internet, linking venerable media organizations and upstart individual accounts into a ready-made conduit for both conventional political messages and outright lies.

Peter Pomerantsev is interested in the geopolitical dimension of modern "influence operations," and his *This Is Not Propaganda: Adventures in the War Against Reality* (PublicAffairs, 2019) is a footloose adventure that jumps from Manila to Mexico City. On his stops, Pomerantsev typically visits academics tracking disinformation flows and activists and civil-society types trying to fight back, frequently invoking his own experience as the son of dissidents who escaped the Soviet Union.

It's worth learning Portuguese (or at least mastering Google Translate) to read Patricia Campos Mello's *A Máquina do Ódio: Notes de Uma Repórter Sobre Fake News e Violência Digital* (Campanha das Letras, 2020). The São

188   Paulo newspaper journalist who broke the story of Jair Bolsonaro's sup-
       porters using WhatsApp groups to spread falsehoods about his opponents
       during the 2018 election, Campos Mello details how questions of online
       disinformation came to dominate Brazilian politics in the following years,
       and how she herself came to be targeted by the "hate machine" of the title for
       reporting on it.

INTRODUCTION

12   **I published a book:** Sasha Issenberg, *The Victory Lab: The Secret Science of Winning Campaigns* (New York: Crown, 2012).

13   **"might as well be":** Stephanie Saul, "Looking, Very Closely, for Voter Fraud," *The New York Times,* September 16, 2012.

13   **along with my Bloomberg colleague:** Joshua Green and Sasha Issenberg, "Inside the Trump Bunker, With 12 Days to Go," *Bloomberg Businessweek,* October 31, 2016.

16   **more than one hundred:** Charles O. Lerche, "Jefferson and the Election of 1800: A Case Study in the Political Smear," *The William and Mary Quarterly* 5, no. 4 (1948): 467–91, https://doi.org/10.2307 /1920636.

16   **Christian Coalition leaflets delivered by mail:** Mike Allen, "Report Tracks Special-Interest Spending," *The Washington Post,* July 18, 2000.

16   **McCain as a godless heathen:** Cal Thomas, "Religious Right Shows in S.C. It's Capable of un-Christian Acts," syndicated column in *Greenville News,* February 23, 2000.

16   **surveys reportedly informed voters:** Richard Gooding, "The Trashing of John McCain," *Vanity Fair,* November 2004.

17   **duped into reporting on forgeries:** Jim Rutenberg, "CBS News Concludes It Was Misled on National Guard Memos, Network Officials Say," *The New York Times,* September 20, 2004.

18   **"You've got to respond":** Alison Mitchell with Frank Bruni, "Spotlight Turns on Ugly Side of Politicking," *The New York Times,* February 11, 2000.

18   **a popular comic:** Randall Munroe, "Duty Calls," *Xkcd,* 2007, https://xkcd.com/386/.

19   **the first substantive announcement:** Steven Nelson, "Trump Vows to Ban Feds from ID-ing Domestic 'Misinformation' if Elected," *New York Post,* December 15, 2022.

20   **defined military activity between nations:** Rupert Smith, *The Utility of Force: The Art of War in the Modern World* (New York: Knopf, 2007).

20   **identified seventeen other countries:** Sanja Kelly, Mai Truong, Adrian Shahbaz, Madeline Earp, and Jessica White, "Freedom on the Net 2017: Manipulating Social Media to Undermine Democracy"

190   (Washington: Freedom House, 2017).

CHAPTER ONE

22 **glimpses of life inside:** Simon Shuster, "Inside the Prison that Beat a President: How Georgia's Saakashvili Lost His Election," *Time*, October 2, 2012.

22 **Videos showed guards torturing:** David M. Herszenhorn, "Unrest Follows Broadcast of Video Showing Prison Abuse in Georgia," *The New York Times*, September 19, 2012.

22 **"Please don't film this":** Giorigi Lomsadze, "Georgia Rocked by Prison Abuse Scandal," Eurasianet, September 19, 2012.

24 **an assessment later confirmed:** Special Counsel's Office, Department of Justice, *Report on the Investigation into Russian Interference in the 2016 Presidential Election*, April 18, 2019.

25 **hyperpartisan content from pop-up outlets:** Dan Abrams, "Now Even Google Search Aiding in Scourge of Fake, Inaccurate News About Election 2016," *Mediaite*, November 13, 2016.

25 **"2016's most disruptive":** John Herman, "Inside Facebook's (Totally Insane, Unintentionally Gigantic, Hyperpartisan) Political-Media Machine," *The New York Times Magazine,* August 24, 2016.

25 **"There is no such thing":** Eric Lubbers, "There Is No Such Thing as the Denver Guardian, Despite that Facebook Post You Saw," *The Denver Post,* November 5, 2016.

25 **a group of teens:** Craig Silverman and Lawrence Alexander, "How Teens in the Balkans Are Duping Trump Supporters with Fake News," *BuzzFeed,* November 3, 2016.

25 **"It was just anybody":** Laura Sydell (host), "We Tracked Down a Fake-News Creator in the Suburbs. Here's What We Learned," *All Things Considered*, National Public Radio, November 23, 2016.

25 **built a company called Disinfomedia:** Jestin Coler, "A Former Fake News Creator on Covering Fake News," Nieman Reports, n.d., https://niemanreports.org/articles/a-former-fake-news-creator-on-covering-fake-news/.

26 **Zuckerberg posted on the site:** Mark Zuckerberg, "I want to share some thoughts on Facebook and the election . . . ," status update, Facebook, November 12, 2016, https://www.facebook.com/zuck/posts/10103253901916271.

27 **wartime incumbent presiding over:** James E. Campbell, "The Presidential Election of 2004: The Fundamentals and the Campaign," *The Forum* 2, no. 4.

27 **ten Vietnam War veterans gathered:** Nina J. Easton, Michael Kranish, Patrick Healy, Glen Johnson, Anne E. Kornblut, and Brian Mooney, "On the Trail of Kerry's Failed Dream," *The Boston Globe,* November 14, 2004.

27 **behind a microphone at the National Press Club:** Stephen Braun, "Crew Contradicted Kerry Over Battle, Doctor Alleges," *The Los Angeles Times,* May 5, 2004.

27 **with a reputed 200 members:** Jodi Wilgoren, "Vietnam Veterans Buy Ads to Attack Kerry," *The New York Times,* August 5, 2004.

28 **assume a clear ideological identity:** Al Tompkins, "How Rush Limbaugh's Rise After the Gutting of the Fairness Doctrine Led to Today's Highly Partisan Media," *Poynter,* February 17, 2021.

28 **first surpassed CNN in ratings:** Andy Meek, "Fox News Channel Has Now Spent 20 Years in the #1 Spot on the Cable News Rankings," *Forbes,* February 1, 2022.

29 **those outlets helped keep the attacks:** Andrew Seifter, "Cables, Right-Wing Radio Ran with Debunked Drudge Charges on Kerry Combat Films," Media Matters for America, July 30, 2004.

29 **began airing a television ad:** CNN.com, "Swift Boat Veterans for Truth: Any Questions," August 5, 2004.

29 **provided journalists an eighteen-page research dossier:** Jodi Wilgoren, "Vietnam Veterans Buy Ads to Attack Kerry," *The New York Times,* August 5, 2004.

29 **his grades as a Yale University undergraduate:** Michael Kranish, "Yale Grades Portray Kerry as a Lackluster Student," *The Boston Globe,* June 7, 2005.

30 **Kerry claimed the ads:** Glen Justice and Jim Rutenberg, "Kerry Is Filing a Complaint Against Swift Boat Group," *The New York Times,* August 21, 2004.

30 **showed 77 percent of Americans:** Mark Schulman, "Kerry Slips Slightly as GOP Heads for NYC," *Time,* August 28, 2004.

31 **together reaching 95 percent:** Darrell M. West, *Air Wars: Television Advertising and Social Media in Election Campaigns, 1952–2016* (Washington: CQ Press, 2017).

31 **first television spot ad aired in 1952:** Stephen C. Wood, "Television's First Political Spot Ad Campaign: Eisenhower Answers America," *Presidential Studies Quarterly* 20, no. 2 (1990), pp. 265–83.

32 **secret research consortium that brought together:** Sasha

192   Issenberg, "Nudge the Vote," *The New York Times Magazine,* October 29, 2010.

33   **reported without any evidence or attribution:** David D. Kirkpatrick, "Feeding Frenzy for a Big Story, Even if It's False," *The New York Times,* January 29, 2007.

33   **amplified *Insight*'s claim to a much broader:** Bill Carter, "Rivals CNN and Fox News Spar Over Obama Report," *The New York Times,* January 24, 2007.

33   **Clinton spokesperson's denial of her campaign's role:** CNN.com, "CNN Debunks False Report About Obama," January 23, 2007.

34   **"We will not be swift-boated":** NBC News, "Obama Debunks Claim About Islamic School," January 25, 2007.

34   **encouraged news organizations to send reporters:** John Vause, "Inside Obama's Alleged Madrassa," Anderson Cooper 360° Blog, CNN.com, January 22, 2007.

34   **see firsthand that the school:** ABC News, "Nothing Extreme About Indonesian School Attended by Obama," January 25, 2007.

34   **"I was kept awake":** Dan Pfeiffer, "Battling the Big Lie: How Fox, Facebook and the MAGA

Media are Destroying America" (New York: Twelve, 2022).

34   **"When I was six":** ABC News, "Nothing Extreme About Indonesian School Attended by Obama," January 25, 2007.

34   **"The hosts violated one of our general rules":** David D. Kirkpatrick, "Feeding Frenzy for a Big Story, Even if It's False."

35   **one piece in a broader fiction:** Trevor Zimmer, "Savage Smeared Obama with False Name, 'Barack Madrassas Obama,'" Media Matters for America, January 11, 2008.

35   **wrote in an October 2007 article:** Ben Smith and Jonathan Martin, "Untraceable E-Mails Spread Obama Rumor," *Politico,* October 13, 2007.

35   **the new lies were able to move:** Patricia A. Turner, "Respecting the Smears: Anti-Obama Folklore Anticipates Fake News," *Journal of American Folklore* 131, no. 522 (October, 2018), pp. 421–425.

36   **assembled its research onto a site:** Marc Ambinder, "Fight the Smears," *The Atlantic,* June 12, 2008.

36   **rumors about his secret origins continued:** Andrew Walzer, "Conservative Media Still Promoting Obama Birth Certificate

Conspiracy Theories," Media Matters for America, June 18, 2009.

37   **launching a prominent fact-checking website:** Elizabeth Flock, "Attack Watch, New Obama Campaign Site to 'Fight Smears,' Becomes Laughing Stock of Conservatives," *The Washington Post,* September 14, 2011.

37   **game enthusiasts on the bulletin-board service 4chan:** Casey Johnston, "Chat Logs Show How 4chan Users Created #GamerGate Controversy," Ars Technica, September 9, 2014.

37   **"open-source reactionary movement":** Joan Donovan, Emily Dreyfuss, and Brian Friedberg, *Meme Wars: The Untold Story of the Online Battles Upending Democracy in America* (New York: Bloomsbury, 2022).

38   **"You can activate that army":** Joshua Green, *Devil's Bargain: Steve Bannon, Donald Trump, and the Storming of the Presidency* (New York: Penguin Press, 2017).

CHAPTER TWO

41   **first by a candidate:** IPN News Agency, "Those Who Propose Something Else Than Joining EU Want Moldvoa to Go Backward, Vlat Filat," November 20, 2013.

43   **Spanish businessman had operated:** Newsroom Panama, "Fake News, Fake Media in Panama Campaigns," June 29, 2017.

43   **media company that had found itself crosswise:** Nestor Corrales, "ABS-CBN on 'Anti-Duterte' TVC: We Are Duty-Bound to Air Legitimate Ad," *Philippine Daily Inquirer,* May 6, 2016

44   **candidacy had been waged belligerently online:** Kate Lamble and Megha Mohan, "Trolls and Triumph: A Digital Battle in the Philippines," December 7, 2016.

44   **compensate for a small campaign budget:** Jodesz Gavilan, "Duterte's P10M Social Media Campaign: Organic, Volunteer-Driven," Rappler, June 1, 2016.

44   **goonish propagandists on a perpetual hunt:** Gerardo Eusebio, "Fake News, Internet Propaganda, and Philippine Elections: 2016 to 2019," Rappler, May 8, 2022.

46   **"If you have a bad actor":** Tara McGowan, "The Fight Against Distrust," *FWIW Podcast,* January 16, 2020.

47   **massive database tracking years of internet traffic:** Wil S. Hylton, "Down the Breitbart Hole," *The New York Times Magazine,* August 16, 2017.

48   **founded and run by longtime Republican admaker:** Jonathan Martin, "GOP Third-Party Effort Nonexistent," *Politico,* June 20, 2008.

194

48 by a twenty-four-year-old Trump supporter: Tess Townsend, "The Bizarre Truth Behind the Biggest Pro-Trump Facebook Hoaxes," *Inc.*, November 21, 2016.

48 "Claims aimed for 'internal' consumption": Robert M. Faris, Hal Roberts, Bruce Etling, Nikki Bourassa, Ethan Zuckerman, and Yochai Benkler, *Partisanship, Propaganda, and Disinformation: Online Media and the 2016 U.S. Presidential Election* (Berkman Klein Center for Internet & Society Research Paper, 2017).

49 Pew Research found just 15 percent: Elisa Shearer and Jeffrey Gottfried, "News Use Across Social Media Platforms 2017," Pew Research Center, 2017.

51 involved in promoting the original legislation: Jeff Bell, "Buckeye Institute (Subtly) Making Case for S.B. 5," *Columbus Business First*, August 24, 2011.

52 chain of like-minded conservative entities: Andy Kroll, "The Right-Wing Network Behind the War on Unions," *Mother Jones*, April 25, 2011.

52 reached beyond the traditional think-tank work: Ed Pilkington and Suzanne Goldenberg, "State Conservative Groups Plan US-Wide Assault on Education, Health and Tax," *The Guardian*, December 5, 2013.

52 unusually active online: Lee Fang, "The Right Leans In," *The Nation*, March 26, 2013.

52 preparing for the next front in a rolling conflict: Heather Gies, "Disaster Averted: How Unions Have Dodged the Blow of Janus (So Far)," *In These Times*, January 10, 2019.

52 argued the union violated his constitutional rights: *Janus v. Am. Fed'n of State, Cnty., & Mun. Emps., Council 31*, 138 S. Ct. 2448, 201 L. Ed. 2d 924 (2018).

CHAPTER THREE

55 seeking to assess heavy investments: Fenit Nirappil, "Why Democrats Care About Virginia's Normally Sleepy House of Delegates Races," *The Washington Post*, November 1, 2017.

55 "How can we take scale-up expertise": Tony Romm, "Reid Hoffman Has Billions of Dollars and One of the Best Networks in Silicon Valley. Here's How He's Using Them to Take on Trump," *Vox*, September 5, 2017.

55 other investors did not panic: Justin Wolfers, "Markets Sent a Strong Signal on Trump . . . Then Changed Their Minds," *The New York Times*, November 18, 2016.

56 *Forbes* estimated his net worth: Mrinalini Krishna,

"LinkedIn Founder Reid Hoffman's Net Worth Jumps $800 Million on News of Sale to Microsoft," *Forbes*, June 13, 2016.

57 job title that had replicated: Betsy Brill and Hilda Vega, "Advisers' Perspective—A Nascent Field But Growing," *Alliance Magazine,* March 2010.

57 "risk-capital or growth-capital arm of the resistance": Tina Nguyen, "The Left's 'Capital Arm of the Resistance': LinkedIn Founder Reid Hoffman Is Spending Hundreds of Millions to Growth-Hack Democracy," *Vanity Fair,* April 30, 2019.

58 "My approach to political investing": Katie Benner, "Using Silicon Valley Tactics, LinkedIn's Founder Is Working to Blunt Trump," *The New York Times,* September 8, 2017.

59 founded in 2014 to inspire self-esteem: Tamara Wilson, "Activist Creates New Narrative to Counter Negative Media Portrayals of Young Black People," CNN, October 9, 2020.

59 generated eye-catching, sometimes highly sexualized: Lachlan Markay, "The Mystery Firms Behind the Liberal Facebook Ads Dubbing a Hawaii Rep a 'CWILF,'" *Daily Beast,* November 20, 2018.

59 apparent goal of assembling right-leaning

Facebook audiences: Alexis C. Madrigal, "The Secretive Organization Quietly Spending Millions on Facebook Political Ads," *The Atlantic,* October 17, 2018.

60 celebrity in political-tech circles: Steven Brill, "Obama's Trauma Team," *Time*, February 27, 2014.

61 "sought to develop technical solutions": Reid Hoffman, "Truth and Politics," Medium, December 26, 2018.

61 had to be determined by a coin flip: Gregory S. Schneider, "A Single Vote Leads to a Rare Tie for Control of the Virginia Legislature," *The Washington Post*, December 19, 2017.

62 saw a big jump in new followers: Howard Koplowitz, "Russian Twitter Bots Invade Roy Moore's Account; Senate Candidate Blames Doug Jones, Dems," AL.com, October 16, 2017.

62 would eventually call for federal authorities: Burgess Everett, "Doug Jones Wants Federal Probe into Disinformation Tactics in His Race," *Politico*, December 20, 2018.

63 beneficiary of other unexpected support: Matt Osborne, "Roy Moore and the Politics of Alcohol in Alabama," LinkedIn, August 9, 2018.

196   63   **from its Twitter account Dry Alabama dispensed:** Dan Cohen [@dancohen3000], "Here are screenshots from the suspended @DryAlabama account," Twitter, January 7, 2019, https://twitter.com/dancohen3000/status/1082378054360539136.

64   **"Y'all's targeting is so wrong":** Elizabeth BeShears [@LizTBeShears], "Y'all's targeting is so wrong, So Wrong #ALPolitics @DryAlabama," Twitter, December 3, 2017, https://twitter.com/LizTBeShears/status/937532119039074304.

64   **end up voting for Jones:** Scott Shane and Alan Blinder, "Democrats Faked Online Push to Outlaw Alcohol in Alabama Race," *The New York Times,* January 7, 2019.

64   **"I was willing to create content":** Ira Glass, "Anything Can Be Anything," *This American Life,* WBEZ, episode 671, March 29, 2019.

64   **"the world's first platform for defending":** Jonathon Morgan, "Introducing New Knowledge: Defending Public Discourse," Medium, November 9, 2017.

65   **prepared in December 2018 to release:** Renee DiResta, Kris Shaffer, Becky Ruppel, David Sullivan, Robert Matney, Ryan Fox, Jonathan Albright, and Ben Johnson, *The Tactics & Tropes of the Internet Research Agency,* report commissioned by U.S. Senate Intelligence Committee, December 17, 2018.

65   **"many of the tactics now understood":** Scott Shane and Alan Blinder, "Secret Experiment in Alabama Senate Race Imitated Russian Tactics," *The New York Times,* December 19, 2018.

66   **asserted a *Daily Caller* headline:** Peter Hasson, "Democrats Ran Russian Bot 'False Flag' Operation in Alabama—and Media Fell for it," *Daily Caller,* December 19, 2018.

66   **Facebook responded to the scrutiny:** Tony Romm and Craig Timberg, "Facebook Suspends Five Accounts, Including that of a Social Media Researcher, for Misleading Tactics in Alabama Election," *The Washington Post,* December 22, 2018.

68   **reputation for being willing to cultivate:** Gabriel Debenedetti, "A 21st Century Breakup," *New York,* September 18, 2019.

68   **"Some tactics are beyond the pale":** Dmitri Melhorn, "Investing in US: 2017–2018 in Review," Medium, December 21, 2018.

CHAPTER FOUR

70   **closed Facebook groups with names like:** Institute for Research & Education on Human Rights, "Breaching the Mainstream: A National Survey of Far-Right Membership in State Legislatures," Appendix C.

70   **any user could search:** Dami Lee, "Facebook is Simplifying Group Privacy Settings and Adding Admin Tools for Safety," *The Verge*, August 14, 2019.

73   **"operatives used targeted advertisements":** U.S. Senate Select Committee on Intelligence, "Russian Active Measures Campaigns and Interference in the 2016 U.S. Elections," November 10, 2020.

74   **"Will 'Deepfakes' Disrupt the Midterm Election?":** Tom Simonite, "Will 'Deepfakes' Disrupt the Midterm Election?" *Wired*, November 1, 2018.

75   **"create confusion about what emails":** Lisa Kaplan, "How Campaigns Can Protect Themselves from Deepfakes, Disinformation, and Social Media Manipulation," *TechTank*, Brookings Institution, January 10, 2019.

76   **manipulated video featuring House Speaker Nancy Pelosi:** Drew Harwell, "Faked Pelosi

Videos, Slowed to Make Her Appear Drunk, Spread Across Social Media," *The Washington Post*, May 24, 2019.

78   **"They see what Breitbart did":** Jason Horowitz, "Steve Bannon is Done Wrecking the American Establishment. Now He Wants to Destroy Europe's," *The New York Times*, March 9, 2018.

78   **"gladiator school for culture warriors":** Chico Harlan, "With Support from Steve Bannon, a Medieval Monastery Could Become a Populist Training Ground," *The Washington Post*, December 25, 2018.

78   **"fundamental building blocks for winning":** Jason Horowitz, "Steve Bannon's 'Movement' Enlists Italy's Most Powerful Politician," *The New York Times*, September 7, 2018.

80   **relevant model was a Democratic Data Exchange:** Reid J. Epstein, "Democrats Belatedly Launch Operation to Share Information on Voters," *The New York Times*, September 6, 2020.

80   **after years of contentious negotiations:** Julie Bykowicz, "Fight Over Voter Data Roils Democrats Ahead of Election," *The Wall Street Journal*, December 15, 2018.

198   80   **also had to contend with an initiative:** Issie Lapowsky, "Alloy Promised Democrats a Data Edge Over Trump. The DNC Didn't Buy It. Now What?" *Protocol*, October 22, 2020.

81   **overcome their reluctance toward sharing:** Alex Thompson, "Democrats Seek Cease-Fire in Voter Data Wars," *Politico*, December 19, 2018.

CHAPTER FIVE

83   **after a 2016 landslide reelection:** Michael Kruse, "The Secret Weapon Democrats Don't Know How to Use," *Politico*, May 12, 2017.

83   **she was appointed to lead:** Simone Pathé, "DCCC Names Cheri Bustos Chairwoman of Heartland Engagement," *Roll Call*, June 27, 2017.

84   **after helping her party take back:** Bridget Bowman and Simone Pathé, "Democrats Look for New DCCC Chair to Protect Majority," *Roll Call*, November 15, 2018.

84   **when it would have to defend:** Laura Barrón-López and Zach Montellaro, "New DCCC Chair Bustos Vows to Stay on Offense in 2020," *Politico*, January 6, 2019.

84   **released a full list of accounts identified:** House Permanent Select Committee on Intelligence,

"Report on Russian Active Measures," March 22, 2018.

84   **begun to detect a swirl:** Debbie Murcarsel-Powell, "Why Did the Florida Latino Community Swing to Trump? It's Complicated," *The Washington Post*, November 27, 2020.

84   **jumping from local talk-radio stations:** Sabrina Rodriguez and Marc Caputo, "This Is F---ing Crazy': Florida Latinos Swamped By Wild Conspiracy Theories," *Politico*, September 14, 2020.

85   **a woman in Queens introduced:** Azi Paybarah, "Stunt Aimed at Ocasio-Cortez Over Climate Change: 'Start Eating Babies,'" *The New York Times*, October 4, 2019.

85   **without any of that essential context:** Angelo Fichera, "Outburst at AOC Town Hall Was Staged," FactCheck.org, October 9, 2019.

88   **expanded their presence in the capital:** Cecilia Kang and Kenneth P. Vogel, "Tech Giants Amass a Lobbying Army for an Epic Washington Battle," *The New York Times*, June 5, 2019.

88   **went to think tanks and interest groups:** Cat Zakrzewski and Elizabeth Dwoskin, "Facebook Quietly Bankrolled Small, Grassroots Groups to Fight Its

Battles in Washington," *The Washington Post*, May 17, 2022.

89 **do more harm to competitors:** Joe Lancaster, "Facebook Welcomes Regulations, Specifically Those That Hurt Its Competition," *Reason*, November 13, 2021.

90 **reduce the rate at which it spread:** Olivia Solon, "Facebook's Plan to Kill Dangerous Fake News Is Ambitious—and Perhaps Impossible," *The Guardian*, July 19, 2018.

90 **difficult for outsiders to assess:** Farjad Manjoo, "What Stays on Facebook and What Goes? The Social Network Cannot Answer," *The New York Times*, July 19, 2018.

91 **no major social-media had a policy:** Kaveh Waddell, "On Social Media, Only Some Lies Are Against the Rules," *Consumer Reports*, August 13, 2020.

91 **religiously and ethnically targeted violence:** Steve Stecklow, "Hatebook: Inside Facebook's Myanmar Operation," Reuters, August 15, 2018.

91 **"with the purpose of contributing":** Sheera Frankel, "Facebook to Remove Misinformation That Leads to Violence," *The New York Times*, July 18, 2018.

91 **list of immediate takedown targets:** Joseph Menn, "Exclusive;

Facebook to Ban Misinformation on Voting in Upcoming U.S. Elections," Reuters, October 15, 2018.

94 **already the biggest single political spender:** Aaron Holmes, "From Trump to Planned Parenthood, These Are the Facebook Pages Spending the Most Money on Political Ads," *Business Insider*, November 14, 2019.

96 **promoted the creation of its Disinformation Task Force:** Caitlin Conant, "2020 Daily Trail Markers: Trump Signs Coronavirus Relief Bill," CBS News, March 27, 2020.

96 **debate over regulation of big tech:** Theodore Schleifer, "The Simmering Debate Over Big Tech Explodes on the Democratic Debate Stage," *Vox*, October 16, 2019.

96 **demanded that Twitter suspend Trump's account:** Donie O'Sullivan, "Kamala Harris Calls on Twitter CEO to Suspend Donald Trump," CNN, October 2, 2019.

96 **struggled in vain to get rivals:** Will Sommer, "Kamala Harris Tries and Fails to Make Trump Twitter Ban an Important Election Issue," *Daily Beast*, October 16, 2019.

97 **voted to impeach Trump:** Dareh Gregorian, "Trump Impeached by the House for Abuse

200   of Power, Obstruction of Congress," NBC News, December 18, 2019.

CHAPTER SIX

100   **retweeted hundreds of times:** Conspirator Norteño [@conspirator0], "The first account to tweet 'The Odessa Shooter's name is Seth Ator, a Democrat Socialist who had a Beto sticker on his truck' was . . ." Twitter, September 1, 2019.

100   **image of a white truck affixed:** Will Weissert and Amanda Seitz, "False Claims Blur Line Between Mass Shootings, 2020 Politics," Associated Press, September 5, 2019.

101   **others were more passive:** Tonya Riley, "2020 Candidates Aren't Sure What to Do About Misinformation," *Mother Jones*, May 27, 2019.

101   **according to one disinformation analyst:** Conspirator Norteño [@conspirator0], "We updated the dataset this afternoon. The claim that the shooter was a Beto-supporting Democrat(ic) Socialist remains . . ." Twitter, September 2, 2019.

101   **researchers at Media Matters identified:** Alex Kaplan, "How Bots and Far-Right Figures Spread a Lie About Beto O'Rourke and the Odessa Shooting," Media Matters for America, September 4, 2019.

102   **O'Rourke would be out of the race:** Patrick Svitek and Emma Platoff, "Beto O'Rourke Drops Out of the Presidential Race," *The Texas Tribune*, November 1, 2019.

102   **"There's value in being more aggressive":** Ryan Lizza, "The Hidden Menace Threatening Democrats' Bid to Beat Trump in 2020," *Politico*, November 15, 2019.

102   **he hired O'Malley Dillon to manage:** Mike Memoli and Lauren Egan, "Joe Biden Names Jen O'Malley Dillion as New Campaign Manager," NBC News, March 12, 2020.

103   **had already become Biden's digital director:** Zach Montellaro, "Biden Picks Up O'Rourke Alum to Lead Digital Efforts," *Politico*, December 12, 2019.

103   **Biden had lagged behind in fundraising:** Sarah Almukhtar, Thomas Kaplan, and Rachel Shorey, "2020 Democrats Went on a Spending Spree in the Final Months of 2019," *The New York Times*, February 1, 2020.

103   **one-quarter as much cash on hand:** Sean McMinn and Alyson Hurt, "Tracking the Money Race Behind the Presidential Primary Campaign," National Public Radio, April 21, 2020.

103   **operate at a severe financial disadvantage:** Shane Goldmacher, "Biden Banks $242 Million as Big-Name Donors write Huge Checks," *The New York Times,* July 16, 2020.

103   **for the first time raised more:** Sarah Ewall-Rice, "For the First Time in 2020, Biden's Monthly Fundraising Haul is Higher than Trump's," CBS News, June 20, 2020.

103   **the Democrat who was setting records:** Amita Kelly, "Biden Announces Record $383 Million September Haul," National Public Radio, October 14, 2020.

103   **eventually raising $365 million in August:** Marc Caputo, "Biden Posts Stunning Monthly Cash Haul," *Politico,* September 2, 2020.

104   **since the 2004 election cycle:** Steve Friess, "The Father of All Web Campaigns," *Politico,* September 30, 2012.

104   **blamed the sexual revolution and other cultural changes:** Kyle Palmer, "McCaskill, Hawley Trade Bards Over Sex Trafficking Comments," WCUR, February 1, 2018.

105   **some took to calling the Malarkey Factory:** Matt Viser, "Inside the 'Malarkey Factory,' Biden's Online War Room," *The Washington Post,* October 19, 2020.

105   **undertook a No Malarkey bus tour:** Matthew Yglesias, "'No Malarkey,' Joe Biden's Unabashedly Lame New Slogan, Explained," *Vox,* December 3, 2019.

107   **some concerned Biden's newly selected running mate:** Samantha Putterman, "The Misinformation Campaign Against Kamala Harris, What You Need to Know," PolitiFact, October 7, 2020.

107   **used with particular effect among Spanish-speaking communities:** Matt Dixon and Gary Fineout, "'I'm Not a F—ing socialist': Florida Democrats Are Having a Post-Election Meltdown," *Politico,* November 17, 2020.

108   **"We all know about Joe's son":** Eric Bradner, "Pam Bondi Attacks Hunter Biden in Speech Filled with Debunked Conspiracies," CNN Politics, August 25, 2020.

108   **fascinated conservative media ever since:** John Solomon, "Joe Biden's 2020 Ukrainian Nightmare: A Closed Probe is Revived," *The Hill,* April 1, 2019.

108   **quest to unearth some sort of corrupt bargain:** Kenneth P. Vogel and Iuliia Mendel, "Biden Faces Conflict of Interest Questions That Are Being Promoted by Trump and Allies," *The New York Times,* May 1, 2019.

202

108 **pursued their own investigation of the Bidens' ties:** Karoun Demirjian, Tom Hamburger, and Paul Sonne, "GOP Senators' Report Calls Hunter Biden's Board Position with Ukraine Firm 'Problematic' But Doesn't Show It Changed U.S. Policy," *The Washington Post*, September 23, 2020.

109 **"The more that we expose":** Kyle Cheney, "Besieged on All Sides, Ron Johnson Says His Probe 'Would Certainly' Help Trump Win Reelection," *Politico*, August 13, 2020.

109 **his father's campaign pushed Twitter:** Cat Zakrzewski and Faiz Siddiqui, "Elon Musk's 'Twitter Files' Ignite Divisions, But Haven't Changed Minds," *The Washington Post,* December 3, 2022.

109 **some cybersecurity and law-enforcement figures then suspected:** Evan Perez, Donie O'Sullivan, and Brian Fung, "No Directive: FBI Agents, Tech Executives Deny Government Ordered Twitter to Suppress Hunter Biden Story," CNN Politics, December 23, 2022.

109 **circulated in right-leaning Facebook pages:** Sharon Kann and Kayla Gogarty, "Right-leaning Facebook Pages Have Been Laying the Groundwork to Attack Kamala Harris Online," Media Matters for America, August 11, 2020.

110 **"Kamala is a cop":** Cameron Joseph, "Progressives Think 'Kamala Is a Cop.' But Cops Hated Harris for Years." *Vice*, August 13, 2020.

111 **like jogging along parade routes:** "Biden Says Trump's July 4 Spectacle 'Misses the Point,' "Associated Press," July 4, 2019.

112 **Fox News article about law-enforcements officials:** Brooke Singman, "More Than 175 Current, Former Law Enforcement Officials Endorse Joe Biden, Slam Trump as 'Lawless' President," Fox News, September 4, 2020.

112 *Wall Street Journal* **op-ed from a retired Navy admiral:** William McRaven, "Biden Will Make America Lead Again," *The Wall Street Journal*, October 19, 2020.

112 **Trump campaign press call featuring Ronny Jackson:** Morgan Chalfant, "Former Trump Doctor Ronny Jackson Questions Biden's Mental Fitness for Office," *Roll Call*, October 13, 2020.

CHAPTER SEVEN

116 **for years the platform's most popular post:** Harsh Clif, "Top 20 Most Upvoted Post on Reddit 2023," QM Games, January 31, 2023.

118 **total number of write-in votes statewide:** Alan Blinder and

Richard Fausset, "Write-In Results from Alabama Senate Race Are In. And They're Downright Weird," *The New York Times*, December 29, 2017.

119 **"we believe strongly that the results":** Tovo Labs, "Proof of Digital Persuasion in Alabama's Senate Race," Medium, April 7, 2018.

119 **often lumped together with the other Alabama campaigns:** Bob Moser, "Interference 2020," *Columbia Journalism Review*, Fall 2019.

119 **a flattering National Public Radio segment:** Alisa Chang and Alex Goldmark, "How to Meddle in an Election," *Planet Money*, NPR, May 24, 2019.

123 **starting almost immediately after Election Day:** Jim Rutenberg, Jo Becker, Eric Lipton, Maggie Haberman, Jonathan Martin, Matthew Rosenberg, and Michael S. Schmidt, "77 Days: Trump's Campaign to Subvert the Election," *The New York Times*, January 31, 2021.

123 **rejected by courts and regulators:** William Cummings, Joey Garrison, and Jim Sergent, "By the Numbers: President Donald Trump's Failed Efforts to Overturn the Election," *USA Today*, January 6, 2021.

124 **using rallies in the state to complain:** Andrew Desiderio and

Matthew Choi, "Trump Uses Georgia Rally to Pressure GOP on Electoral College Challenge," *Politico*, January 5, 2021.

124 **"He told them their votes didn't count":** Alex Isenstadt, "McConnell Allies Blame Trump for Georgia," *Politico*, January 6, 2021.

124 **"They didn't want to vote":** Grace Panetta and Eliza Relman, "Trump Said He Didn't Go All-Out to Push Republicans to Vote in the Georgia Senate Runoffs Because He Was 'Angry' Over Losing the Election, Book Says," *Insider*, October 19, 2021.

125 **ransacked offices and smashed historic furniture:** Devon Link, "Fact Check: Photo Shows U.S. Capitol Cleanup After Rioters Left American Flag Among Debris," *USA Today*, February 3, 2021.

125 **died as a result of the hours-long siege:** Chris Cameron, "These Are the People Who Died in Connection with the Capitol Riot," *The New York Times*, January 5, 2022.

125 **what was dubbed "the Big Lie":** Caleb Ecarma, "New CNN Chief Wants Anchors to Say Goodbye to 'the Big Lie,'" *Vanity Fair*, June 16, 2022.

125 **"It would never come into their heads":** Adolf Hitler, *Mein*

204   *Kampf,* translated by James Murphy (London: Hurst and Blackett, 1939).

131   **"are putting litter boxes in schools":** Sharon Sullivan, "'They Are Putting Litter Boxes in Schools for People Who Identify as Cats,' Says Boebert. 'Not True,' Responds Durango School District," *Colorado Times Recorder*, October 4, 2022.

CHAPTER EIGHT

133   **"The slave was freed in '88":** Tribunal Superior Eleitoral, *Eleição de 1933: O Limiar da Justiça Eleitoral,* online exhibition, 2021.

133   **too remotely to be served by traditional polling places:** Thomas Fujiwara, "Voting Technology, Political Responsiveness, and Infant Health: Evidence from Brazil," *Econometrica* 83, no. 2 (March 2015).

134   **number of ballots left blank:** Jairo Nicolau, "Impact of Electronic Voting Machines on Blank Votes and Null Votes in Brazilian Elections in 1998," *Brazilian Political Science Review* 9, no. 3 (December 2015).

134   **"our election system has advanced":** Stephen Buckley, "Brazilians' Pride Grows in Electronic Voting System," *The Washington Post*, December 2, 2000.

134   **tapped to design a new headquarters:** Agencia O Globo,

"TSE Gastará R$ 335 Milhões Em Nova Sede, Projetada Por Niemeyer," March 25, 2007.

134   **now houses nearly a thousand:** *Consultor Jurídico,* "Nova Sede do Tribunal Superior Eleitoral Será Inaugurada," December 8, 2011.

135   **Brasilia's jet-age city plan was designed:** Danilo Matoso Macedo and Sylvia Fischer, "Brasilia: Preservation of a Modern City," *Conservation Perspectives,* Spring 2013.

135   **blast hundreds of millions of unsolicited:** Patrícia Campos Mello, "Empresários Bancam Campanha Contra o PT Pelo WhatsApp," *Folha de São Paulo*, October 18, 2018.

135   **went unreported to authorities:** Patrícia Campos Mello, "Empresários Bancam Campanha Contra o PT Pelo WhatsApp."

136   **57 percent of Brazilians said:** "Datafolha: Quantos Eleitores de Cada Candidato Usam Redes Sociais, Leem e Compartilham Notícias Sobre Política," G1, March 10, 2018.

136   **collected 100,000 political images:** Cristina Tardáguila, Fabricio Benevenuto, and Pablo Ortellado, "Fake News Is Poisoning Brazilian Politics. Whats App Can Stop It," *The New York Times*, October 17, 2018.

136 **used WhatsApp to disseminate this material:** Gabriel Ferreira and João Pedro Soares, "Como Functiona a Máquina de WhatsApp Que Pode Eleger Bolsonaro," *Época,* October 24, 2018.

136 **scans of traditional leaflets to original memes:** Francisco Brito Cruz, Heloísa Massaro, Ester Borges, "'Leaflets,' Memes, and Chain Messages: An Exploratory Study About Spam Received on WhatsApp During the Brazilian Elections," *InternetLab,* May 17, 2019.

137 **determining the nipple was a real item:** "'Mamadeiras Eróticas' Não Foram Distribuídas Em Creches Pelo PT," Projecto Comprova, September 27, 2018.

137 **one congresswoman allegedly maintained:** Philip Reeves, "Brazil's President Draws Controversy Over Covert Use of Cyberspace," *Morning Edition,* National Public Radio, December 17, 2019.

138 **opened a much-hyped "election war room":** Sheera Frankel and Mike Isaac, "Inside Facebook's Election 'War Room,'" *The New York Times,* September 19, 2018.

138 **festooning the walls with American and Brazilian flags:** Casey Newton, "Inside Facebook's Election War Room," *The Verge,* October 18, 2018.

139 **works for left-wing candidates nationwide:** Paulo Maneira, "Marqueteiro de Boulos Vai à Bahia Para Ajudar Pré-Candidates a Deputado e ao Senado," *Bahia Jornal,* April 22, 2022.

139 **confronting Bolsonaro at the start:** "Boulos vs Bolsonaro: 'All of Brasil Knows You're Male Chauvinist, Racist and Homophobic," Brasilwire, August 10, 2018.

140 **saw himself being characterized as a "marketer":** Lucas Franco, "Marqueteiro de Boulos Planeja 'Campanha Antidepressiva' na Bahia," *A Tarde,* April 28, 2022.

140 **on acres owned by Volkswagen:** "Filósofo, Líder Dos Sem-Teto Saiu de Casa Para Ser Militante," *Folha de São Paulo,* July 5, 2014.

140 **"take over tracts of land":** Guilherme Boulos, interviewed by Mario Sergio Conti, "Struggles of the Roofless," *New Left Review,* July/August 2021.

142 **Supreme Court opened an investigation:** Carolina Brígido, "Toffoli Determina Abertura de Inquérito Para Investigar Notícias Falsas Sobre o STF," *O Globo,* March 14, 2019.

206

142 **issued a one-page order citing little:** "Toffoli Abre Inquérito Para Apurar Notícias Falsas Contra o Supremo," *Migalhas*, March 14, 2019.

143 **"Complain at will, criticize at will":** Renan Araújo, "Brazilian Supreme Court Inquiry Into 'Fake News' Violates Freedom of Speech," OxHRH Blog, May 20, 2019.

143 **he saw Bolsonaro and his sons:** Ricardo Brandt and Rafaela Vivas, "Moraes no TSE: Desafio de Frear Conflitos e Defender as Urnas," *SBT News*, August 15, 2022.

144 **documents journalists determined were authentic:** "Revista Censurada por STF Diz Que Ministro Aplicou Multa de R$ 100 Mil," *Folha de São Paulo*, April 15, 2019

144 **issued an order giving the minister:** Andréia Sadi, "Moraes Determina Que Weintraub Seja Ouvido Pela PF Para Explicar Fala em Reunião Ministerial," G1, May 26, 2020.

144 **suggesting an unproven link between vaccines:** Debora Alvares, "Brazil's Bolsonaro Investigated for Linking Vaccine and AIDS," Associated Press, December 3, 2021.

144 **de Moraes opened an inquiry into that:** BBC News, "Bolsonaro: Brazilian Supreme Court Opens Investigation into Vaccine Comments," December 4, 2021.

144 **had his home raided:** BBC News, "Os Argumentos do STF Para Decretar a Prisão Do Ex-Deputado Roberto Jefferson," August 13, 2021.

144 **"criminal hate speech contrary to democratic institutions":** Lucas Valença, Fabio de Mello Castanho, and Thaís Augusto, "Roberto Jefferson É Preso Pela PF, Após Determinação de Alexandre de Moraes," UOL, August 13, 2021.

144 **"It cannot be allowed":** Carolina Brígido, "'Pode Espernear à Vontade,' Diz Alexandre de Moraes Sobre Inquérito Para Apurar Ataques ao STF," *O Globo*, March 19, 2019.

145 **he identified eleven criminal offenses:** Hermínio Bernardo, "Moraes Inclui Bolsonaro Como Investigado No Inquérito das Fake News," *My News*, August 4, 2021.

145 **the country's dictatorship-era national-security law:** Veridiana Alimonti, "Brazil's Bill Repealing National Security Law Has Its Own Threats to Free Expression," Electronic Frontier Foundation, April 30, 2021.

145 **"Justice is blind but":** "Justice de Moraes Fears Digital Militias Will Spread Fake News

Ahead of 2022 Elections in Brazil," MercoPress, October 29, 2021.

145 as a substitute judge, then a full member: "Brazil's Superior Electoral Court Has New Chief Judge," Agência Brasil, August 17, 2022.

146 flew to the mid-sized industrial city: Carol Delgado, Victória Jenz, and Fellype Alberto, "Bolsonaro Lança Campanha em Juiz de Fora com Discurso Focado na Agenda Conservadora," G1, August 16, 2022.

146 "giving thanks for the second life": Guilherme Grandi, "No Primeiro Dia de Campanha, Jair Bolsonaro Volta a Juiz de Fora e Discursa a Apoiadores," *Gazeta de Povo*, August 16, 2022.

146 had publicly called a "scoundrel": "Bolsonaro Sobe o Tom e Ataca Alexandre de Moraes: 'Deixa de Ser Canalha,'" SBT News, September 7, 2021.

146 Brasilia news site published leaked transcripts: Guilherme Amado, "Exclusivo. Empresários Bolsonaristas Defendem Golpe de Estado Caso Lula Seja Eleito; Veja Zaps," *Metrópoles*, August 17, 2022.

146 de Moraes had their offices raided: Jack Nicas and André Spigariol, "To Defend Democracy, Is Brazil's Top Court Going Too Far?" *The New York Times*, September 26, 2022.

148 which was unusually central in Brazilian life: Fernanda Saboia, "The Rise of WhatsApp in Brazil Is About More Than Just Messaging," *Harvard Business Review*, April 15, 2016.

148 it was fifty-five times more expensive: "Tech and Media Outlook 2016," Activate, October 19, 2015.

149 the messaging app Telegram: Darren Loucaides, "How Telegram Became the Anti-Facebook, *Wired*, March 2022.

149 run from Dubai by its two Russian founders: Matt Binder, "What You Need to Know About Telegram, the WhatsApp Alternative," Mashable, January 26, 2021.

149 participated only after being threatened: Laís Martins, "Brazil's Electoral Court Brings Platforms Closer Ahead of Presidential Elections, But Questions Over Companies' Commitments Remain," Global Voices, September 20, 2022.

150 traced its authority to regulate content: Gustavo Ferreira Sanots, "Redes Sociais, Desinformação e Regulação do Processo Eleitoral: Um Estudo Baseado na Experência Eleitoral Brasiliera de 2018," *Revista de Investigações Constitucionais* 7, no. 2 (May/August 2020).

208   150   **coauthor of the 2019 book:**
Francisco Brito Cruz et al., *Direito
Eleitoral na Era Digital* (Belo
Horizonte: Casa do Direito, 2019).

150   **dozens of proposals
circulated:** Francisco Brito Cruz
and Mariana Valente, "Leis Para
Desinformação Exigem Mais do
Que Boas Intenções," *Nexo Jornal*,
May 15, 2020.

151   **months before taking office,
de Moraes had asserted:** Estadão
Conteúdo, "Moraes Diz Que TSE
Pode Cassar Registro de Candidato
que Divulgar Fake News," *Istoé*,
June 1, 2022.

151   **not think of either a
comic-book hero:** "O Imrpovável
Culto a Alexandre de Moraes,"
Meteoro Brasil, YouTube,
August 25, 2022.

151   **or Bond villain, depending
on one's perspective:** Leonardo
Desideri, "'É Como Um Vilão de
James Bond,' Diz CEO do Gettr
Sobre Alexandre de Moraes," *Gazeta
do Povo*, September 11, 2021.

151   **issued an injunction against
using footage:** Ricardo Della
Colletta and Mateus Vargas, "TSE
Proibe Bolsonaro de Usar na
Campanha Discurso em Residencia
Official em Londres," *Folha de São
Paulo*, September 20, 2022.

151   **"could hurt the equality of
conditions":** "Bolsonaro Barred
from Using UN General Assembly
Speech in Campaign Ads," The
Brazilian Report, September 22,
2022.

151   **newspapers counted the
number of court "actions":**
Eleições 2022 newsletter, "Reta
Final nos Estados," *Folha de São
Paulo*, September 27, 2022.

153   **promoted by the pop singer
Anitta:** Camilla Freitas, "Com Anitta
e Mais Damosos, Brasil Se Mobiliza
Pelo Voto de Adolescentes," *Ecoa
UOL*, March 25, 2022.

153   **then by American actors:**
"Hulk, Luke Skywalker, DiCaprio:
Quem Está Por Trás da Campanha
Para Jovens Título de Eleitor,"
Gazeta de Povo, April 5, 2022.

153   **two million sixteen- and
seventeen-year-olds:** "TSE Data
Shows Last-Minute Vote
Registration of 2 Million Young
People," *Folha de São Paulo*, May 6,
2022.

153   **increasing their share of the
electorate:** Joan Royo Gual, "Why
Brazil's First-Time Voters Are
Backing Lula," *El País*, October 1,
2022.

154   **Satanist with ties to
organized crime:** Anthony Faiola
and Gabriela Sá Pessoa, "The
Cannibal v. the Satanist: Toxic
Politics Is Poisoning Brazil," *The
Washington Post*, October 28, 2022.

154   **carefully cultivated digital
presence:** Rich Brown and Martina

Graña, "5 Viral Moments from a New Era in Latin American Politics," *Americas Quarterly*, October 25, 2022.

154 biggest stars of the Brazilian left: Nivaldo Souza, "Quen é Guilherme Boulos, que Chega a Câmara Mirando a Prefeitura de São Paulo," *Jota*, October 28, 2022.

155 received fifteen different filings: "Federação Brasil da Esperança Apresenta ao TSE 15 Ações Contra Notícias Falsas," *Consultor Jurídico*, August 24, 2022.

156 when de Moraes declined to do so: Andréia Sadi, "Bolsonaro Queria Radicalizar e Propor Adiar Eleição; Sem Apoio, Recua e Antecipa Terceiro Turno," *G1*, October 26, 2022.

156 ordered a federal police investigation: Emily Behnke, "Torres Pede Abertura de Inquérito Sobre Site 'Bolsonaro.com.br,'" *Poder360*, August 31, 2022.

156 the new, largely satirical site: "Site 'Bolsonaro.com.br' Exibe Críticas ao Presidente," *Poder360*, August 31, 2022.

156 Bolsonaro significantly overperformed polls: André Spigariol and Jack Nicas, "Brazil's Polls Were Wrong. Now the Right Wants to Criminalize Them," *The New York Times*, October 24, 2022.

156 top congressional allies introduced: Cedê Silva, "House

Fast-Tracks Bill to Penalize Pollsters," *Brazilian Report*, October 19, 2022.

157 groundless claims portraying him as hostile: Ranier Bragon, "Lula Informa ao TSE Ter Criado Perfis Nas Redes Sociais Direcionados a Evangélicos," *Folha de São Paulo*, August 20, 2022.

157 his favored terrain of economic policy: Catia Seabra, Julia Chaib, Victoria Azevedo, "Lula Foca Combate à Fome, Busca Evangélicos e Tenta Conte Avanço de Bolsonaro," *Folha de São Paulo*, August 15, 2022.

157 serving as Lula's liaison to other evangelicals: Anna Virginia Ballousier, "Quem é o Pastor que o PT Chamou Para Ajudar Lula com os Evangélicos," *Folha de São Paulo*, February 13, 2022.

157 having his lawyer challenge Twitter: "Advogados Recorrem de Decisão do TSE que Manteve Post que Liga Lula ao PCC," *UOL*, August 21, 2022.

157 "invasions of churches and prosecution": Agência Estado, "Lula Vai ao TSE Contra Posts que o Ligam a 'Invasão de Igrejas' e PCC," *Correio Braziliense*, August 21, 2022.

158 court ruled in his favor: Caroline Oliveira, "TSE Manda Excluir Posts Que Ligam Lula a Invasão de Igrejas e Ciro Gomes à

210 Violência de Gênero," *Brasil de Fato*, September 6, 2022.

CHAPTER NINE

159 **video-sharing platform that promoted itself:** Andrew R. C. Marshall and Joseph Tanfani, "New Breed of Video Sites Thrives on Misinformation and Hate," Reuters, August 22, 2022.

161 **"restoring trust in information":** Peter White, "Meghan, The Duchess of Sussex's Debut Podcast Set for Summer on Spotify as Royal Duo Continue to Tackle Misinformation," *Deadline*, March 17, 2022.

162 **was quoted by the BBC:** Marianna Spring, "US Midterms: How BBC's Voter Profiles Were Shown Hate and Disinformation Online," BBC News, November 7, 2022.

162 **always shifting responsibility back:** Ashley Gold, "Groups Demand Crackdown on Online Misinformation Ahead of Midterms," *Axios*, October 26, 2022.

163 **appeared in the newspaper's business section:** Nico Grant, "YouTube May Have Misinformation Blind Spots, Researchers Say," *The New York Times*, November 5, 2022.

163 **personally handed to the commander-in-chief:** Charlie

Savage, "What Is the President's Daily Brief?" *The New York Times*, December 12, 2018.

168 **having its criminal-investigative division speak:** Tobias Burns, "GOP Under Fire for Rhetoric Over IRS," *The Hill*, August 13, 2022.

169 **most-shared articles on Facebook:** Benedict Nicholson, "These Were the Top Publishers of June 2020 on Facebook," NewsWhip, July 23, 2020.

169 **baseless claim Floyd had died:** Eamon Whalen, "Candace Owens Exposes Only Herself in Her BLM Documentary," *Mother Jones*, March/April 2023.

169 **death had been faked:** Davey Alba, "Misinformation About George Floyd Protests Surges on Social Media," *The New York Times*, June 1, 2020.

171 **Bully Pulpit Interactive began marketing:** Aleda Stam, "Tech Talk with Bully Pulpit Interactive's Danny Franklin," *PR Week*, December 8, 2020.

171 **"To better arm our clients":** Jessica Reis and Joe Ste. Marie, "Combatting Disinformation with 'Parry,'" Bully Pulpit Interactive, Medium, January 25, 2021.

171 **tested fifteen narratives that were raising doubts:** Joe Bonfiglio and Jessica Reis, "The

Disinformation Battlefield—Narrative Over Facts," *Morning Consult*, May 12, 2021.

172 **"Misinformation is an existential threat"**: Dan Rather, *Dan Rather's America*, SiriusXM, November 29, 2016.

176 **shut out of battleground-state offices:** Nick Corasaniti, Reid J. Epstein, and Jonathan Weisman, "Election Denial Didn't Play as Well as Republicans Hoped," *The New York Times*, November 9, 2022.

177 **Meta did in Ireland alone:** Cianan Brennan, "Facebook's Irish Staff 'Really Stressed' Ahead of Reported Layoffs," *Irish Examiner*, November 8, 2022.

179 **non-political content to build digital audiences:** Theodore Schleifer, "Tech Billionaires Are Plotting Sweeping, Secret Plans to Boost Joe Biden," *Vox*, May 27, 2020.

180 **raised more than $20 million:** Brian Schwartz, "Dark Money Group Launches $2 Million Pressure Campaign on Moderate Lawmakers to Pass Parts of Biden's Agenda," CNBC, May 18, 2021.

181 **lead massive rallies, parades, and military displays:** Marcia Reverdosa, Rodrigo Pedroso, and Camilo Rocha, "As Brazil's Military Rolls Out the Tanks for Independence Day, Bolsonaro Tells Fans to 'Make a Stand,'" CNN, September 7, 2022.

182 **president never conceded:** Ricardo Brito, Brian Ellsworth, and Rodrigo Viga Gaier, "Brazil's Bolsonaro Does Not Concede to Lula, But Authorizes Transition," Reuters, November 1, 2022.

183 **a thirty-three-year-old trash-picker and recycling activist:** Tom Phillips, "'This Nightmare Is Over': Lula Vows to Pull Brazil Out of Bolsonaro's Era of 'Devastation,'" *The Guardian*, January 1, 2023.

183 **on TikTok videos and in Twitter posts:** Jack Nicas and Simon Romero, "'We Will Die for Brazil': How a Far-Right Mob Tried to Oust Lula," *The New York Times*, January 13, 2023.

183 **rampaging through the buildings:** Jack Nicas and André Spigariol, "Bolsonaro Supporters Lay Siege to Brazil's Capital," *The New York Times*, January 8, 2023.

183 **subsequent siege lasted for hours:** Katie Polglase, Gianluca Mezzofiore, Tara John, and Rodrigo Pedroso, "'Command Your Troops, Damn It!' How a Series of Security Failures Opened a Path to Insurrection in Brazil," CNN, January 14, 2023.

Columbia Global Reports is a nonprofit publishing imprint from Columbia University that commissions authors to produce works of original thinking and on-site reporting from all over the world, on a wide range of topics. Our books are short—novella-length and readable in a few hours—but ambitious. They offer new ways of looking at and understanding the major issues of our time. Most readers are curious and busy. Our books are for them.

If this book changed the way you look at the world, and if you would like to support our mission, consider making a gift to help us share new ideas and stories.

Visit globalreports.columbia.edu to support our upcoming books, subscribe to our newsletter, and learn more. Thank you for being part of our community of readers.